LIFE'S LITTLE ANNOYANCES

LIFE'S LITTLE ANNOYANCES

True Tales of People

Who Just Can't Take It Anymore

IAN URBINA

Times Books
Henry Holt and Company
New York

Times Books
Henry Holt and Company, LLC
Publishers since 1866
175 Fifth Avenue
New York, New York 10010

Henry Holt® *is a registered trademark of Henry Holt and Company, LLC.*

ISBN-0-7394-6225-3

Designed by Meryl Sussman Levavi

Printed in the United States of America

To Aidan, for making me laugh like no one else can.

CONTENTS

Contents

CHAPTER 6. VEHICULAR MISANTHROPY 105

CHAPTER 7. RAGE AGAINST THE MACHINE 123

CHAPTER 8. BILLS, BANKS, AND BILE 149

Contents

CHAPTER 9. TURNABOUT IS FAIR PLAY 167

INTRODUCTION

Most days the job ended late. My exhausted trek back home from the *New York Times* building in Times Square often didn't start until after 9 P.M.

But keeping me in forward motion during that foggy stumble was the simple and intense pleasure that awaited me back at my apartment: a pint of Ben & Jerry's ice cream.

I prefer Heath Bar Crunch. The bodega on the corner sold Cookies and Cream, which contented me just fine.

With kids and a wife back in Washington, D.C., I had little interest in laying down roots while working in Manhattan during the week. In searching for a place to rent, I had three simple criteria: it needed to be inexpensive, not too costly, and affordable. At $350 a month, the closet I found met my needs perfectly.

It was a three-story walk-up shared by two women, one of whom had a boyfriend who stayed there most of the time. With opposite schedules, the four of us rarely crossed paths, and everyone seemed to like it that way.

Still, living in close quarters brings friction—and much of it I could do nothing to avoid. For example, it was far too awkward—and maybe also a bit unfair—for me to complain about the personal noises coming late at night from the adjacent room used by my apartment mate and her boyfriend. So I kept my mouth shut. And while I couldn't help but be annoyed at the flecks of kitty litter that the apartment's two cats habitually left on my pillows while I was at work, I knew better than to try to reason on such matters with a feline lover.

But when the ice cream started disappearing, we had big problems.

It started humbly. Avoiding deep gashes that might attract notice, the culprit skimmed off the top with gentle strokes of a spoon. Soon, the strokes were more aggressive, and a third of the pint would disappear overnight. When the perpetrator began leaving only one spoonful after a late-night binge to avoid having to throw the container away, I decided that something had to be done.

I tried everything. Hiding the pint behind the stacked ice trays did not slow the culprit down. The same was true for writing my name across the top of the container. I was reluctant to leave a note on the refrigerator—"Attention: Midnight Marauder"—because I thought it would appear too ornery without any guarantee of success. Asking each apartment mate individually required scheduling and it couldn't help but seem accusatory to the innocent.

So, as I sat at the kitchen table one night, stewing over my predicament and staring in frustration at the vacant depths of a pint that yesterday was practically full, a simple solution caught my eye.

Salt.

Crystalline and white, it would camouflage beautifully with Cookies and Cream. Natural and edible, it would also avoid sickness, not to mention a lawsuit, if unwittingly consumed.

It was perfect.

Just the idea was cathartic. And in harboring it for several days, I found a restored pep in my stride on my daily walk home as I flirted with the decision of whether tonight was the night.

Yes, it risked burning a bridge with at least one of my apartment mates. But some bridges are meant for kindling. I had already resolved that I was not going to buy any more ice cream than what I could eat during the walk home, so I was relatively immune from revenge. At worst, the tactic would jolt the culprit in much the same way that I was jolted on a regular basis. At best, it might also anger the marauder into dropping the cloak of anonymity.

So, two weeks before I planned to move out of the apartment, I set the bait. It was a newly opened container of Cookies and Cream, a quarter inch skimmed off the top, capped by a thin but solid layer of salt. To test the invisibility of my trap, I stood at the freezer, spoon in hand, and adjusted the lighting to various levels.

It was foolproof.

Several days passed, and then the e-mail came. As I had suspected, the culprit was the roommate with the boyfriend. She was livid and—perhaps rightly—she accused me of taking my ice cream way too seriously. Indignant at the passive aggression in my actions, she gave an explanation for her behavior that was as self-righteous as it was lame: she said that she had a near-pathological weak spot for ice cream and that if it was anywhere within reach she had no way of resisting it. She seemed surprised that I wasn't more sympathetic to her condition.

The e-mail tirades stopped a couple of days later, and I moved out soon after that. But the more I reflected, the more I was struck by two things in her reaction to the whole incident.

At no point did she pause to concede the pure genius of my booby trap. Sure, a mouthful of salt stings. But anyone—most of all a culprit who had been warned with ice tray barriers and my name written across the pint—would have to admit the cleverness in finding an effective yet innocuous way to turn the tables.

But even stranger was her pejorative use of the

term "passive-aggressive." In my view, criticizing something for being passive-aggressive is like faulting a tactic for being discreet. Just as there are times when subtlety is the worst approach, there are also times when passive aggression is the best.

In fact, the more I talked to friends about similar experiences—sometimes in dealing with roommates or neighbors, but most often in dealing with larger and faceless adversaries—the more I realized that passive aggression is actually the vehicle for a noteworthy array of scrappy ingenuity.

The stories people offered on the topic were enough to fill a book. And they did.

Less creative souls—like myself—exacted sweet but gentle revenge. Others mined the occasions for art or profit. Some opted for circumvention. A few people stood firm, adopting perfectly irrational yet strangely cathartic ways to convey their dissent.

But why focus on such petty behavior? The answer is simple: Because it is the stuff of everyday survival. And our myriad coping mechanisms offer a clear window onto the complicated mix of humor, anger, creativity, and irrationality that makes us all so human.

That loud cell phone talkers or inconsiderate dog owners who do not clean up after their pets raise our blood pressure faster than the atrocities in Darfur or the growing national debt does not imply that we are callous to the suffering of others—though certainly some people are. The reason is simply that some realities are closer than others, and it's difficult to focus on Darfur and whatever else when your co-worker in the adjacent cubicle is noisily playing video games.

How we choose to deal with these grievances gives our personalities definition and a valuable edge. They are formative for exactly the reason that no one likes a Pollyanna: Happy-go-lucky people are boring and predictable.

The easygoing sorts will be quick to point out that only fools make mountains out of molehills. And to some degree, they will be right. Nevertheless, these same laid-back folks will be lying if they try to pretend that they are above the fray.

One need only watch the angry gesticulations of that driver with the "Don't Sweat the Small Stuff" bumper sticker after he gets cut off in traffic to recognize a basic truth about the human condition:

No one is above life's little annoyances.

1

WEAPONS OF THE WEAK

It makes no sense that inconsiderate dog owners refuse to clean up after their pets, so why should the response be any more rational? If a person risks getting shot by taking the logical approach to dealing with impatient drivers who lay on their horns for no apparent reason, then why not try a softer, and perhaps less reasonable, tactic?

The world would be an awfully boring place if everyone acted logically. And justice would only belong to the litigious.

Thankfully, there are people who occupy the space just below aggression but just above following the rules.

So when our favorite TV program is interrupted by yet another fund-raising telethon, it's these types who call in to unnerve the smiling phone attendants seated in front of the cameras. And when every waiting room on the planet seems to have a television blaring some mind-numbing talk show, these people bring us the perfect tool to shut them off without anyone knowing who did it.

They are the arms dealers and foot soldiers of life's smallest battles. And we all owe them a debt of gratitude. They make the world safe for the rest of us who are equally frustrated but just a little more timid.

WHO TURNED THIS THING ON, ANYWAY?

Nothing tortures the psyche more than being trapped in a room with the voice of Geraldo Rivera lecturing about the decline of American culture. And no matter how hard you try to look away from that television in the hospital waiting room or the airport lobby, the babbling entrances you like the rest of the zombies sitting around.

If only you could turn it off without causing a minor uproar—or at least without anyone knowing it was you who did it.

All Mitch Altman wanted to do that day was catch up with several friends he met for dinner. "The whole point was for us to share each other's company," says the forty-eight-year-old inventor, who lives in San Francisco.

But the televisions perched in the corners of the Chinese restaurant were monopolizing attention. "No one could focus back on each other," Altman says.

When Altman and his friends finally did reclaim control of their attention, the conversation quickly drifted to the topic of public television sets. All agreed that a discreet and universal remote would be the ultimate weapon against this pervasive annoyance.

So Altman built one. And after testing it out at a couple of local bars and restaurants, he named his pocket-sized gadget "TV-B-Gone" and began selling it on the Internet.

"The choice of having that distraction on or not should be yours," he says. "Now, it can't be taken for granted that everyone wants the television blaring."

Of course, his weapon cuts both ways. "It has only one button," Altman explains. "Unfortunately, that means it works as well to turn on the TV as it does to turn it off."

HONK IF YOU HATE THIS STORE

David Terry says that he is not prone to moralizing, but the presence of the adult video store down on the main drag annoys him nonetheless.

"It's poorly kept and just plain ugly," he says. "It's basically a cinder block bunker with a door and it sticks out even in an area with only gas stations and a strip mall."

Terry has no pull with local officials in his New Jersey town, and he hardly has the time or inclination to raise a stink with the local zoning board.

He can, however, honk his horn. And that is what he does every time he drives by. When he passes the store and sees a customer leaving or entering, he gives a little friendly toot on his horn and waves enthusiastically.

"It works like a charm," he says, explaining that his action usually sends a patron scrambling to his car or into the store while nervously glancing over his shoulder.

Terry says he takes keen delight in imagining what thoughts must dart through each patron's head: Was that my mom? Oh no, I think my boss drives that kind of car! Maybe that was my wife? "It's simple but harmless," he says.

A DOG OWNER'S ULTIMATE CRIME

Inconsiderate dog owners commit countless crimes against humanity.

They let their nosy canine off the leash and force the rest of us to fend for ourselves as Fido sniffs our every imaginable crevice. They leave their four-legged fiend home alone to yap incessantly as everyone within earshot stews about the things we would like to do to shut the dog up.

But the worst offense of all is when they fail to pick up after their furry friend.

For Merlyn Kline, this is a constant source of tension. His mother lives in Exeter, England, near a public park where dog owners rarely pick up their mess. "She goes on about it day in and day out," says Kline, who is forty-two years old and owns a software company there. "She finds it absolutely appalling because it ruins the park for everyone else."

One day as his mother bellyached about the topic, Mr. Kline began entertaining himself by constructing small flags out of toothpicks and fluorescent tape. He was trapped at the kitchen table anyway, he thought, so why not do something distracting? After making a batch of the miniature flags, it struck him that he should put them to use. So the next time he was walking in the nearby park he stuck a flag in each turd he found. His mother began doing the same.

"Seems silly, really," Kline says. "But I can tell you that I have seen dog owners on several occasions look over at flags and act chagrined. I think it draws attention to the problem."

Susan Lulic lives on the other side of the Atlantic Ocean. But, oddly, she came up with a similar approach to handling the problem.

Lulic carries a canister of gold paint with her when she takes her dog out for a walk early in the morning. When she comes across an unclaimed mound, she gives her canister a quick shake and spray paints it.

Why?

"It gives a little pizzazz to a boring walk," she says. "It also signals to everyone that some rude bastard did not do his civic duty."

Lulic, who lives in Tucson, Arizona, and teaches adult basic education and GED classes to people who have run into problems with the law, says that she adopted her artistic approach several years ago after a dog owner let his dog leave a deposit at the top of her driveway. She spray painted it and stuck a small flag in the top that said "Pick Up Your Shit," hoping the owner would see it the next time he passed by.

No one ever picked up the mound, but someone did later leave a reply note in the turd. "Let's just say it was threatening enough language that I decided to let them have the last word," Lulic says.

WHEN PLEDGE DRIVES GET IN THE WAY

If you are looking forward to a certain television show, the last thing you want to see in its place is a stage full of people asking you to call now and make a donation.

For Mark Thomas this is a frequent frustration. As a professional pianist, Thomas looks forward to the concert specials regularly televised by the Public Broadcasting Service. But every so often, he sits down to catch a concert only to find that the station is airing its seasonal pledge drive instead.

"I can't tell you how annoying it was," says Thomas, who is thirty-seven years old and lives in Queens, New York. "Sometimes I had rushed home to watch something that I had been looking forward to all week."

With time to kill, Thomas decided to reap his revenge by making the phone-a-thon just a little bit more interactive. At first, he just called and hung up over and over again. "I got a kick out of hearing one of the droning announcers say 'We want to hear more of that. More phones ringing,' " he says.

But soon he upped the ante and tried to rattle the volunteers seated on stage. After dialing he would speak gibberish and watch the facial expression of the volunteer for signs of bafflement.

"The best was when the camera happened to be

focused closely on the person I was calling," he says. "I would say, 'I can seeeee yooouuu,' and then describe what they looked like."

Taking pity on the volunteers, Thomas says that he no longer uses the tactic. "But I still laugh to this day about it," he says. "When I turned off my TV each time at the end of the evening, I felt like I had certainly gotten my fill of entertainment."

BREAKING INTO FORT KNOX IS EASIER

Brian McCracken left the store with three new CDs and raced home to listen to them. But when he got to his stereo, the frustrating ritual began.

First, he tried using his fingernails. But they glided over the cellophane as if it were glass. Then he resorted to using his teeth, but they were not exacting enough to grasp the slight ruffle in the packaging. Next, he headed to the kitchen knife drawer. The options there had more chance of slicing his finger than of cutting the thin layer of CD packaging. In the end, he opted for brute force and scraped his nails across the top of the case.

At the time, he owned over three thousand CDs. "That's a lot of times to experience this frustration," says the forty-four-year-old software designer from San Clemente, California. "It used to make me so tense that I would have a tough time unwinding again."

Finally, McCracken cobbled together a solution—a razor encased by plastic. This simple device cuts through CD packaging without risk of slicing a finger. "It was great because listening to music no longer required this crazy process anymore," he says.

McCracken now sells his simple contraption through a CD-accessory product line called MacTec Products. "I guess a lot of people have stopped going to their knife drawer," he says.

HONKU

Only saints and deaf people have never been tempted to throw an egg at a car with a driver needlessly laying on his horn. Aaron Naparstek, on the other hand, faced this temptation daily.

Naparstek lived in an apartment in Brooklyn near the corner of Clinton and Pacific streets. Virtually every day during the morning rush, the intersection backed up. "It was a perfect storm of honking," says the thirty-five-year-old freelance writer. "Everything came together at this corner."

Cabbies used the route regularly to get to midtown Manhattan. Ambulances took the street to get to a nearby hospital. And the lights were timed in such a way that the intersection regularly gridlocked. "Practically every several minutes someone was sitting on their horn," Naparstek says. "And this is 6 a.m., mind you."

Then one day, he snapped.

From his third-floor window, he fired three eggs in rapid succession at a particularly aggressive horn honker. The first hit the trunk, the second the roof, the third the windshield. Emerging from his car, the driver yelled some things that scared the bejesus out of Naparstek.

"He seemed really serious," he recalls. "I realized I was taking my life in my hands and that I had better find another way to cope with this."

Thus was born the Honku.

From that point forward, whenever Mr. Naparstek heard people needlessly honk their horn, he penned a little poem. Three lines, totaling seventeen syllables and written in a five-seven-five format, his haikus brought him relief. They were simple creations, and like most haikus they usually derived from a direct observation of something in nature that led to a sense of Zen. His first read:

> You from New Jersey
> honking in front of my house
> in your SUV

Later ones took a heavier tone:

> Terrorism is
> a Lincoln Continental
> leaning on the horn

Naparstek began taping his haikus to the light pole nearest to where the honk had occurred. Before long, other people joined the act. One that Naparstek came across while walking down the street was:

Oh, Jeezus Chrysler
what's all the damned honking Ford?
please shut the truck up!

Then they started appearing all over New York City. "People started writing me with their own haikus about every urban annoyance imaginable," he says. "The guy who parked too far from the hydrant and took up two spaces, the person who never picks up their dog's poop, they were all there." The most common were haikus about car alarms.

Eventually, Naparstek put the best ones in a book. "I still write them," he says, adding that he rarely posts them on light poles anymore. "This city has enough honking to keep me going for a long time."

A GENTLE WAY TO TELL SOMEONE
TO GET LOST

The idea came to him while he was out one night with his friends, at a local bar. Jeff Goldblatt, a twenty-eight-year-old business student at Emory University in Atlanta, watched as a pudgy guy with one too many Coronas under his belt tried to put the moves on a knockout blonde standing in the corner.

At first, Goldblatt and his friends felt bad for the girl. It must be a real pain to have to deal with such pushiness, they thought. But their sympathies shifted when the girl went overboard and began yelling and making a scene even after the guy had clearly gotten the hint. "We began debating within our group whether there was a more humane way for the girl to have given the message," Goldblatt says. "We couldn't come to an agreement on a method that would have allowed her to fend the guy off while also allowing him to save face."

But Goldblatt soon thought of a solution.

As a joke, he activated an unused voice mailbox from a spare phone line in his house to record a message for incoming calls.

"You've reached the rejection hotline," the recording said in the cheesiest voice Goldblatt could muster. "You're hearing this message because the person who gave you this number was not interested in receiving your call. Don't take it personally but . . ." He e-mailed the friends who had participated in the discussion at the bar and told them the number to call.

They thought it was hilarious. So they began e-mailing the number to other friends. And before long so many calls were coming in that the voice mail line crashed his phone provider's computer system.

"It was unbelievable," Goldblatt says. "Web sites were posting it, radio DJs were mentioning it. The line couldn't handle the calls."

Realizing that he had struck a chord, Goldblatt erected a Web site. He also bought additional phone numbers—paid for out of his own pocket—with area codes in various major cities. "It just seemed like an effective way to deal with a common problem, so it was worth the expense to me," he says.

Mr. Goldblatt's Web site now offers "rejection" phone numbers in twenty-eight cities. All told, they receive 1.6 million calls per month. "That's a lot of rejection," he says.

Had the knockout blonde in the bar that night wanted to be extra careful, she probably would have brought Goldblatt's phone number with her. She might also have brought Josh Santangelo's e-mail address as well.

Santangelo invented papernapkin.net to provide a little extra protection against unwanted suitors. Write any name in front of @papernapkin.net, and the person who e-mails the address will automatically get a rejection response. "The person who gave you this e-mail address does not want to have anything to do with you," the reply e-mail says, continuing with a long explanation of possible reasons for the rejection. "We have no beef with you and we'd be just as pleased to serve your rejection needs as we are to serve anybody else."

Santangelo, a twenty-six-year-old Web developer from Seattle, Washington, said that he thought of the idea after hearing about the rejection phone line. He reports that more than thirty thousand people e-mailed it within its first month of service in August 2004.

In contrast to Jeff Goldblatt's rejection phone line, the stakes are much higher when a person uses Josh Santangelo's e-mail service. If a suitor's come-on e-mail is sappy or strange enough, Santangelo removes the names from it and posts the contents on his Web site.

"There are a lot of people who just won't take no for an answer," Santangelo says. "It can't hurt to have extra ways to fend them off."

WHEN FLYING BECOMES A TEST
OF WILLS AND WITS

All Dan Cabacungan wanted to do was sit back and take a nap, and instead he got into a two-hour battle of wills with the passenger seated behind him. All Ira Goldman wanted to do was use his laptop and place his drink on his tray table, and instead he got bashed in the knees. Air travel these days is beginning to look like a pro wrestling smackdown.

Dan Cabacungan describes himself as a fairly laid-back guy. He wasn't asking for much on that flight back home after a grueling week of travel. "It was a Friday night and I hadn't slept for thirty hours," he says. "All I wanted was a tiny bit of shut-eye."

So, after waiting for the plane to reach altitude, Cabacungan snuggled into position, tucked his minuscule pillow into the crook of his neck, and slowly began to recline his seat. But suddenly, an inch and a half into its angle, the seat stopped reclining. Perplexed, Cabacungan figured that perhaps something within the chair's mechanism was hitting a snag. He leaned forward and tried again. But it wasn't budging.

Realizing that it was the passenger behind him, Cabacungan slowly unbuckled his seatbelt and turned around to shoot a quizzical and annoyed look. The man in the seat behind shot back a "get lost" look and said that he was trying to use his laptop. "I've given up enough space already," the passenger said.

Cabacungan says that he flies often enough to know the basics of flight etiquette and this wasn't it. "With my ticket I buy not just the seat but the ability to relax in it," he remembers thinking.

But he said nothing to the man, opting instead to try to make do and take a nap with the space he had. No such luck. He was too distracted by how tense he was getting over the other passenger's encroachment.

So he commenced with low-grade warfare.

First, he began applying steady pressure on the seat, pushing discreetly enough that it might just feel like weight but forcefully enough to wear down his adversary. When that didn't work, he waited until the slightest sign of turbulence and made the most of it. "I kept jiggling long after the plane had leveled," he says. The passenger behind him seemed unfazed.

Then Cabacungan tried another tactic: like a careful fly fisherman, he gently began casting his seat forward and back, over and over again. "I think this got me a centimeter in the end," he says.

Exhausted, Cabacungan gave up. "I had no other ideas except to ask the flight attendant to arbitrate," he says. "I really didn't want to resort to that because it seemed too easy and childish." So he sat quietly, pondering his defeat and wondering whether there was any truth to those New Age reports he had read about

people who could do harm to others by simply pro-
jecting bad vibes. He tried to channel his negative
thoughts at the man.

Suddenly, nature intervened.

As Cabacungan lay still, he felt his enemy getting
up from his seat to go to the bathroom. He watched in
quiet glee as the man headed up the aisle, and with pure
delight he leaned his seat back. "When the guy came
back, I had to pretend to be sleeping to contain my vic-
torious laughter," he says.

Had the passenger with the laptop been Ira
Goldman, things might have ended differently.

"I'm 6'3" and I used to fly close to sixty thousand
miles per year," says Goldman, a lawyer who was a policy adviser to California governor Pete Wilson in the
1990s. "When people recline in front of you and you're
the tall guy, life is miserable."

On one flight Goldman couldn't take it anymore,
and he jammed his umbrella in the crook of the arm of
his tray table to prevent the woman in the seat in front
of him from reclining and bashing his knees. This
inspired him to create the Knee Defender, which consists of two small plastic wedges that a passenger can
attach to his tray table to serve the same purpose as
Goldman's umbrella. He put the devices on the market
in September 2003 and has sold over ten thousand of
them for about $15 a pair.

"This is defense for the tall guy, not some sort of

revenge," he says, adding that the Federal Aviation Administration has said that there is no safety ruling that bars them.

Most of the people who write to him about his product say that they prefer the more civil approach of kindly asking the person to limit his recline. "But in the end they realize the limits of etiquette," he says.

Be that as it may, Ira Goldman will probably want to wait on going to the loo if he is seated behind Dan Cabacungan.

2

❦

SERVICE WITH A SNARL

The salesman is stalking you like a dog in heat because he wants his commission. The cashier says she needs your full name, home phone number, and zip code, even though all you are buying is a pack of AA batteries. You have to learn a special lingo just to order a small coffee.

Shopping isn't annoying for the money you have to fork over. It's annoying for all the other things involved in the transaction.

And yet opting out of commerce altogether is tough. So you make the best of it and try to hustle in, make your purchase, and hustle out.

But some people give a little extra, and the result is priceless.

"NO, SERIOUSLY, I'M JUST BROWSING, THANKS"

If you are unlucky enough to enter the orbit of a pushy sales clerk, casual browsing can start to feel like being shadowed by a stalker. "Is there anything I can help you with?" he says with a fake smile. "Well, if you need me, I'll be right here."

Every aisle you go to, there he is. And if you pause for too long or stare at a rack too intently, he jumps in with a comment about how great the item is and which styles are on sale.

That's why David Hord never leaves his Toronto home without his special MasterCard. Even though the card has been inactive since 1998, he says he still uses it regularly whenever he encounters a salesperson who won't take no for an answer.

"If I say, 'I'm just looking,' or 'I'll find you when I need you,' I really do mean it," he says.

As a regular buyer of stereo and computer equipment, Hord often shops at technology stores, where he says the commission-seeking is most aggressive. And when salespeople pester him, he usually gives them three chances to back off. But if one of them keeps stalking, he heads directly to the most expensive section of the store, making sure the salesman stays in tow.

"I often go with a theme," he explains. "If they've

followed me into the stereo section I might start with a small stereo system, but now I need something that will play MP3s, and once I have that I need batteries—oh, and memory cards."

As the dollar signs begin appearing in the sales clerk's eyes, Hord charges forward.

"And will my computer be able to handle this new MP3 player?" he asks. "No? Well, better get a laptop that's strong enough to handle it."

And on it goes.

After about half an hour, Hord heads to the nearest register. The sales clerk usually volunteers to carry his pile of loot. Once all the items are entered into the computer, Hord hands the cashier his special MasterCard.

"This is expired," the cashier says.

"Really, when?" Hord replies quizzically.

"Uh, seven years ago, sir," the cashier responds, equally confused.

"Oh, darn," Hord says, before adding that he will have to come back another time. He then walks out, usually with the salesperson staring in disbelief.

"Sure, it's mean," he says. "But it gets the point across." And when he wants to be extra sure that his message is clear, he tosses a parting shot. He turns to the pushy salesman and says, "Well, I did tell you three times that I was just browsing. Next time, I guess you'll believe me."

A MEDIUM COFFEE, HOLD THE LINGO

Sometimes the terms seem pretentious or boastful. Other times they are misleading or even belittling. But marketing is nothing if not an attempt to bend the way we think and speak. And while all companies put great thought into how they pitch their goods, some companies push the lingo too far.

That's when customers start bucking.

Seth Shepsle goes to Starbucks regularly, but he usually asks for a "medium" because he finds "grande" —as the coffee company calls the size—simply too annoying. "Their wording is ridiculously pretentious," says Shepsle, who is twenty-eight years old and works for a theater company in Manhattan.

Andrew Kirk likes to order from Domino's Pizza. But when he is not too hungry, he makes a point of requesting a "small," even though he knows that he will be corrected and told that "medium" is the smallest available size. "It makes me feel better to point out that their word games aren't fooling anyone," says Kirk, a twenty-four-year-old freelance writer from Brooklyn.

Starbucks coffee is too bitter for James Arinello's tastes. He goes to Dunkin' Donuts instead. But even there, he runs into problems. "It's incredible to me that no one ever advised the people at Dunkin' Donuts that calling their largest coffee 'The Great One' might be a little bit silly," says Arinello, a twenty-four-year-old graduate student in theology at Boston College. "To ask for it using their term makes me feel like I have to subjugate myself to a cup of coffee, which is just ridiculous." He said he just requests an "extra large" and that most everyone knows what he is talking about.

Movie theaters, restaurants, and grocery stores aren't much better.

"I'm thirty years old so I don't see why I need to ask for a 'child size' to get the small size drink at my local movie theater," says Janine Papp, a grant writer for a nonprofit group in Manhattan. Popcorn is no better. "If I order a 'small' I'll be getting a medium-sized bag," she reports, saying that she usually just asks for the "smallest possible bag" of popcorn instead.

Occasionally, the hang-ups get bizarre.

"Chicken fajitas" hardly seems like a contentious term to most. But Rose McGraff says that her late husband used to rant regularly about the name. "I ain't eating any goldang chicken fajitas. There ain't no such thang," he would say. "Fajitas are charcoal grilled flank steak. I know chickens inside and out, and they ain't got no flanks on 'em anywheres." Having raised show chickens in southern Oklahoma for fifteen years, Mr. McGraff probably knew what he was talking about.

Diana Kaell shares the frustration with fake food names and she curtails her diet accordingly. A fifty-

two-year-old research coordinator who works in a doc-
tor's office in Setauket, New York, Kaell refuses to
order Chilean sea bass in restaurants because it is rarely
from Chile. The same goes for Kobe beef; it is illegal to
serve in the United States, but it is still on some upscale
menus, she reports, despite the fact that it is rarely ever
from Kobe, Japan.

"To me, it makes no sense," she says. "Why not
just call things like they actually are?"

DELOCATOR

Out shopping, Christine Hanson had time to kill while a friend tried on a couple of outfits. So she decided to grab a quick cup of coffee. But she didn't want Starbucks.

"My philosophy has always been that if you don't like Starbucks, then don't go there," she says. "Easier said than done."

Out the front door of the clothing store and to the right: there was a Starbucks. Up the block and to the left: there was another.

Sometimes finding a cup of non-Starbucks coffee is like finding a parking space in midtown Manhattan. God forbid if you want a cup of coffee that is also not from some other big corporate chain.

"And this was in SoHo," says Hanson, a thirty-year-old multimedia professor at Los Angeles Mission College. "It's supposed to be a neighborhood with a reputation for being alternative and creative."

After failing to find a non-Starbucks coffee house, Ms. Hanson settled on a grande. But the annoyance stuck with her for days.

Eventually she sat down at her computer and invented the Delocator, a Web site where any Starbucks hater can enter a zip code and find out where the nearest independent coffee house is located.

Launched in April 2005, the Web site has received more than two million visitors.

"I don't hate the company. Actually, I worked as a barista for them one summer," Hanson says. "But after seeing them shut down my favorite coffee shop in Somerville, Massachusetts, I started noticing their presence everywhere and it really started to bother me."

Coffee houses are supposed to be creative sanctuaries, she explains, but that becomes impossible if they all become the same.

CONFUSING THE SUPERMARKET SPIES

Even a quick run to the grocery store has become an opportunity for companies to invade our privacy. Every store now seems to have its own discount card, which means shoppers can either pay higher prices or let the companies use the cards to collect data about their buying habits.

Rob Carlson resents having to make this choice.

"It should be enough that you are a loyal customer," he says. "I can't help but wonder about that famous story about the guy who slipped in the supermarket." As the story goes, a customer slipped and fell while shopping in a grocery store aisle and then sued the grocery store. When the case went to trial, the lawyer for the grocery store chain used the customer's purchasing data to argue that the customer probably fell because of his drinking habits.

"It may be an urban legend," Carlson says. "But I don't think I want to take chances."

So Carlson takes the precaution of using other people's discount cards.

After realizing that despite the presence of three bar codes on most discount cards, store clerks only check the one on the back of the card, Carlson began printing his own bar codes using a program he found on the Internet. Rather than using fake numbers on the bar code, he uses the numbers from someone else's card. "That causes the most amount of scrambling of the store's data," he explained.

But finding other people who might want to swap their discount card number can be difficult, so Carlson created "Rob's Giant BonusCard Swap Meet," a Web page where people swap their own card numbers online. Swappers still get the benefit of all the major discounts offered at the register, but they also get the added perk of confusing the company's data miners. Since Carlson lives in the Baltimore area, where he works as a Web programmer, and he only shops at Giant supermarkets, his site is limited to customers with Giant cards.

However, some stores have caught on, Carlson says. Many discount cards now offer fewer cash discounts and more deals that are tied directly to a person's buying record. Rather than offering fifty cents off a gallon jug of milk, many cards now offer a free gallon of milk after the customer's record shows that she has bought five gallons over the past two months.

"These folks aren't stupid," says Carlson. "They have a lot of incentive to try to get information on us."

Rob Cockerman shares Rob Carlson's concerns.

"It's bad enough facing the cashier with my cart full of vodka and fish sticks," says Cockerman, a print designer who lives in Sacramento, California, and shops at Safeway. "Will someone someday realize that

I only buy ice cream after midnight? If I buy condoms one month, and a pregnancy test the next, does some kind of red flag get raised?"

But rather than scramble his grocery store's data, Cockerman likes to flood it.

After registering a new card using his real name and address, he carefully photographed his card and printed the bar code and number onto a sheet of address labels. He then put a request on his personal Web site for everyone who wanted to help him become Safeway's Ultimate Shopper: "If you shop at Safeway, I need your assistance in creating an army . . . an army of clones. Together we might amass a profile of the single greatest shopper in the history of mankind." Drop him an e-mail, he said, and he would mail a copy of his bar code to be attached to another person's card. Those who participated would still get savings from their cards, but they would miss out on the odd promotions that the store offers from time to time.

People e-mailed him from as far away as Fairbanks, Alaska, and Washington, D.C. "The reaction was incredible," he says, estimating that about 250 people are shopping under his name.

Of course, a far simpler tactic is to sign up with an alias when registering for a discount card. But where is the fun in that?

BREAKING THEIR SCRIPT

The girl behind the counter at Baskin-Robbins certainly heard Mark Thomas when he said, "One scoop of Rocky Road in a cup to go, please." Yet she insisted on asking: "Will that be one scoop or two?" And then: "Cup or cone?" followed by: "Will you be having that here or to go?"

The service representative on the phone had no idea how to solve David Wallach's problem. But before ending the conversation the representative nonetheless said, "I'm glad we could be of service. Is there anything else I can help you with?"

To survive mindless jobs, many people shift to autopilot. And increasingly, companies are attempting to ensure quality in customer service by crafting rigid scripts that their representatives have to follow.

But to be on the other side of these conversations can feel like talking to a robot, and not a very helpful one at that.

"It's tough to break people's routine, I guess," says Thomas, the professional pianist from Queens, New York, who also has a peeve about pledge drives on public television. (See page 9.) "But it can get tedious if you're the other person."

Thomas says that his response is to just keep saying the same sentence over and over again until the clerk realizes that there is no point going through the list of standard questions.

When Ben Bynum runs into the same predicament, he strikes back by making more work for the clerk.

"Wait, maybe I will get something different today," he says. "But I don't have my contacts in so could you read the options to me?"

One by one, he makes the clerk go down the list. "It usually wakes them up," says Bynum, a twenty-three-year-old musician from Port Jefferson, New York.

Stewart Dean finds it galling when a customer service representative asks him whether there is anything else she can do for him even when she hasn't done anything for him in the first place. To lash back, he requests something that he is sure the person on the phone can't possibly provide.

"I usually respond: 'Sure. Would you please get Bush out of the White House?'" says Dean, a fifty-seven-year-old computer administrator for Bard College in Annandale-on-Hudson, New York.

David Wallach finds this pro forma question exasperating as well. "How can you help me with anything else if you haven't even helped me at all yet?" he usually replies. Wallach, a twenty-five-year-old computer programmer living in Queens, New York, observes that the rigidity of these scripts can lead to fairly ridiculous situations, like the one that unfolded during a recent call he made to Verizon. After a customer service representative was unable to solve Wallach's problem, he asked to speak with a supervisor. The representative asked if she could put him on hold first.

"Do I have a choice?" he replied.

The representative said that in order for her to get a supervisor, she needed to put him on hold.

"Well, do what you must," Wallach responded.

The representative asked again, "So can I put you on hold?"

Wallach repeated his original answer, only to be followed with the same question again from the representative. Suddenly, it dawned on him: the representative needed an explicit yes or no to proceed. So he decided to say anything but those two words.

"Do what you must," he said. And around they went.

"Sure," he replied. And around they went again.

"Go right ahead." One more time they went.

Finally, the representative broke the loop.

"I need you to confirm that I can put you on hold—yes or no," she said.

This time, Wallach replied by explaining that "sure" and "go right ahead" essentially mean the same thing as one of the two words she was seeking. Those alternative responses will just have to suffice, he said. Realizing that she was going to have to go off script to break the cycle, the representative handed Wallach to the supervisor.

"The whole purpose of these policies is to make the representatives more helpful," he says. "Yet they accomplish just the opposite."

CHEATING THE EXPRESS AISLE

There is always someone who cheats the system and never thinks twice about it. And then that person runs into Chris Baker at the supermarket.

Baker has a habit of making small purchases. Therefore, he is often in the express checkout line at his local supermarket, which is for people with "15 items or less" in their cart. Invariably, there is a guy also in line who thinks he can get away with buying twenty.

That's when Baker switches into what he calls "Sesame Street mode."

He begins by counting loudly and clearly as he loads each of his own items onto the conveyer belt. "It's just subtle enough that there is room for people to think that you are doing it for your own sake," says the twenty-eight-year-old graphic artist from Summerville, South Carolina. "But it's also just obvious enough for the guilty person and anyone else with a clue to know you are making a point."

Baker says that he has yet to shame anyone into actually leaving the express line. But he is not done trying.

"It's always the guilty party who looks the other way and pretends it's not happening," he says. "And it's usually the clerk who tosses me a knowing glance and chuckles a bit."

TRUTH OR DARE IN CREDIT CARD SIGNATURES

It's one thing for a waiter to hand the man the check after a meal. Far worse is when the waiter won't even let the woman sign the receipt on her own credit card.

Barry L. Ritholtz and his wife, Wendy, know this frustration all too well.

After a pleasant meal at a restaurant, Wendy Ritholtz says that she is almost always the one to gesture to the waiter, signaling for the check. Removing her credit card from her purse, she will review the charges on the bill and place the credit card inside the small folder for the waiter to pick up. But when the waiter returns with the receipt for a signature, he almost always hands it to her husband to sign.

"She had been the one to hand it over and the card quite clearly had her name on it," Barry says. Still the waiter usually slides the book to Barry, leaving Wendy, a high school teacher, quietly fuming across the table. "I could have been on bended knee next to the table shining her shoes and they still would hand me the receipt," he observes.

Whenever Wendy vented about the obvious sexism involved, Barry would listen patiently and nod in agreement. When she was done he would usually respond with a sympathetic shrug and a simple statement—"I have the penis," he would say. This would usually send Wendy into another fit of rage.

Each and every time this happened at a restaurant, Barry would chuckle about his own private joke, because as he offered his simplistic response to his wife, he also wrote the same four words in the signature box of the credit card receipt.

"I wrote it legibly in cursive," says Barry, who is the chief market strategist for an investment bank in New York City. "Never once was I questioned." He kept the joke to himself for years, until one night when Wendy was getting especially worked up over the topic. He then slid the yellow carbon copy of the receipt across the table.

Laughing at first, Wendy then scolded her husband. "They might notice," she said in a hushed tone.

"Well they haven't noticed any time over the past twelve years," he replied. "Why should they notice now?"

Incredulous, Wendy checked her old credit card receipts when she got home. Surely enough, he had been signing the receipts that way for years.

"You really know that no one is looking at these things if neither the waitress nor my wife ever once caught on," Barry says.

To make a point, Matthew Siers has never signed his credit card receipt. But he shares the suspicion that no one ever checks the signatures, and that ticks him off. "It's a hollow exercise," he says. "It has always felt like a completely false sense of security."

So one day, the twenty-six-year-old high school economics teacher from Foley, Minnesota, turned to his students to help test his theory. After getting permission from their parents, he sent several students into various local stores and used their parents' credit cards to buy expensive items. When the students were asked to sign the electronic pad to verify their credit card purchase, they signed everything but their names.

One student drew a small flower on the keypad. Another wrote "Madonna." A third put an "X." No one was questioned by a cashier.

"I think we were all blown away by what we had just pulled off," he says.

T. C. Lin is hardly surprised because he has been proving this point for years.

As someone with Caucasian features, Lin is the last person that sales clerks expect to sign his credit card receipt using Chinese characters. (He is a thirty-six-year-old independent filmmaker who lives in Taipei, Taiwan, but visits the United States occasionally.) Most clerks don't even notice when he does, but when they do, it usually triggers a perplexed look. If they ask for further identification, he whips out his Republic of China identification card, which has no English on it.

"I personally don't see how someone can replicate their own signature exactly each time under any circumstance," says Lin. "And I'm pretty sure the clerks at the checkout aren't signature forgery experts."

ROAD RAGE IN THE SUPERMARKET AISLE

It is the simplest of courtesies, which is why it is so strange that few people follow it.

When shopping at the grocery store, people should park their carts to the side of the aisle before venturing off. Otherwise, the cart becomes the responsibility of the next person, who has to stop what she is doing to move it out of the way.

"Some people have this sense of endowment," says Allan Doeksen. "Either that or they're just oblivious."

But rather than getting mad, Doeksen channels his road rage.

When he first arrives at the grocery store, Doeksen tosses a couple of items into his cart. Some are private or mildly embarrassing, such as condoms. Others are just expensive, such as shaving razor refills, which can cost up to $10 for a small box. All are small and easily planted.

When he encounters someone rudely blocking traffic, Doeksen calmly moves the unattended cart. But before he returns to his cart, he discreetly drops several of his special items into the other person's pile.

"It's the small price I impose," says Doeksen, a twenty-six-year-old secretary at a hospital in Chicago. "The same type of person who leaves their cart like that will probably not notice the added item until they get home."

THE CASHIER'S SPELLING BEE

Woe be unto the cashier who dares to ask Jonathan Wren for his name and personal information.

"They don't need this data," says the biology and computer science research professor at the University of Oklahoma. "And I don't see why they have to request it." So he imposes an on-the-spot spelling bee on the pesky sales clerk. The exchange goes as follows:

"May I have your name?" the cashier asks.

"Ghossein Dhatsghabyfaird-Johnson," Wren replies.

The cashier glances in confusion before asking, "How do you spell that?"

"With a hyphen," Wren clarifies.

"Once more?" the cashier asks.

"Ghossein Dhatsghabyfaird-Johnson." (Wren once had a colleague whose name was Ghossein Dhatsghabyfaird, and the "Johnson" is added for good measure.)

"Could you please spell that?" the cashier asks, glancing at the half dozen people waiting behind Wren in line.

"Oh . . . just like it sounds," he says nonchalantly.

Typing in "Johnson," the cashier moves on and asks for Wren's address.

"Washburn, Wisconsin, 14701 Northeast Wachatanoobee Parkway, Complex 3, Building O, Apartment 1382b," he replies. As the cashier is almost done typing in the address, he adds, "Or did you mean current address?"

Stopping, the cashier says with clear frustration, "Yes. Current address."

"Diluthian Heights, Mississippi, 1372 South Tinatonabee Avenue, Building 14C, Suite 2, Box 138201," Wren replies slowly.

The cashier types in the new address when Wren suddenly interjects, "No, wait, it's *North* Tinatonabee Avenue." Annoyed, the cashier backs up the cursor and changes the line.

"I think," Wren mumbles with a quizzical look on his face.

When he is feeling especially cruel, he takes the game into overtime. Waiting until the cashier asks, "Is all the information you gave correct?" a standard question at many stores, he responds, "Of course not," adding that his real name is on the credit card receipt the cashier just handed him.

Wren says that he recognizes that it is not the cashiers who set policy. The point, rather, is to get managers to see that this information gathering is backing up the line.

"It's a little mean, I must admit, but no jury would convict me," he says.

3

❦

OCCUPATIONAL HAZARDS

The co-worker in the adjacent cubicle always leaves her cell phone at her desk, and when she goes to meetings the cutesy ring tone goes off all day with no one to answer it.

The co-worker on the other side plays video games on his computer nonstop, leaving it up to everyone else to pick up the slack.

Another colleague has a habit of sticking his hand in your bag of cookies when you are away from your desk.

Even if you ignore the lousy wages and the drudgery of routine, work can be a trying place. But getting the job was hard enough, so you find ways to cope.

Once in a while there is a chance to do something about it. Who would let this chance get away?

USING INSTANT MESSENGER
FOR SABOTAGE

One of Scott Alexander's co-workers is a slacker. He plays video games on his computer during most of their shift. Sometimes it's Tetris. Other times it's Solitaire.

"Meanwhile, I'm left scrambling around handling every call that comes in," says Alexander, who is thirty-six and works for a Pennsylvania computer company. "Plus, the sound effects drive me nuts."

While Alexander is not the type to bother his boss with such a small matter, he is also not the type to pass up a challenge.

"I wanted to get back at him in some lower-grade fashion," he says.

Alexander and this co-worker sit in adjacent cubicles with a wall in between. On the shelf above Alexander's desk is a spare monitor that he has positioned perfectly so that he can always see a reflection of his colleague's computer screen and can see what he is doing. Throughout the day, Alexander keeps an eye on his co-worker's activities, and whenever a game is going particularly well, he sends his co-worker an instant message from an anonymous account that he has set up for just this purpose.

"He isn't too bright," Alexander says, "so he hasn't figured out how to keep new instant messages from popping to the top of the screen." The second or two it takes the co-worker to click "NO" or "CANCEL" to make the pop-up go away is just enough time to ruin a game.

The best part is that the tactic has succeeded in getting the co-worker caught on several occasions by his manager.

And even though the co-worker has a small camera attached to the top of his computer to tip him off when the manager approaches, he struggles to close the game because of the instant-message boxes that always seem to pop up when the manager comes around.

"Really, I can't imagine a better form of sabotage," Alexander says.

THE ART OF DEMOTIVATION

Platitudes are bad enough. But motivational platitudes are the worst, especially when they come with cheesy photographs on the posters that adorn the walls of so many corporate conference rooms.

"Attitude determines altitude," E. L. Kersten quotes derisively. "What really does that mean? The truth is that you could have a great attitude but still be basically incompetent."

Kersten first grew sick of these inspirational aphorisms in 1998 while he was working at an Internet start-up. "They kept trying to pump us up and wow us with company excitement even though the company was tanking," he recalls. "The speeches and the posters were all a distraction from answering straight questions and solving real problems."

So Kersten and two equally disgruntled colleagues began creating their own motivational posters. Using pictures they found in magazines and elsewhere, they added subtitles that offered a more honest—if also a bit jaded—view on life.

"Get To Work," said a subtitle beneath a photo of the crystalline lake with a crew team rowing, "You're not being paid to believe in the power of your dreams."

A poster with runners sprinting around the track offered a similarly barbed rendition of the truth.

"Defeat," it said. "For every winner there are dozens of losers. Odds are that you're one of them."

After pinning their homemade creations at their desks, Kersten saw that they were getting noticed—and drawing chuckles and nods—from colleagues. Before long, he and his two friends decided to market their bitter pills.

The resulting company, Despair Inc., has become a multimillion-dollar mockery of the so-called "successories" industry. Plastering his acerbic doses of reality onto mugs, sticky pads, calendars, and posters, Kersten has even published a book titled *The Art of Demotivation*.

"The whole industry of these self-help and inspirational products stems from a self-indulgent culture that basically tells people confronted with real failure to retreat to self and stoke the fires of narcissism," Kersten says. "We give a fuller picture of the truth and a bit of humor to go with it."

THE JOB APPLICATION LETTER

Few things are more demoralizing than writing job application letters.

"There you are trying at once to write something that shows that you fit in," says Joey Comeau, "while at the same time you're trying to show you're different."

Comeau knows this agony well. After the dot-com bubble, he lost his job as a computer programmer and he began sending out ten to fifteen letters per day. "There is nothing worse than trying to sell yourself to a stranger," he says. "For me, it went on for month after month."

After diligently sending out the letters and receiving no responses, Comeau finally decided to see whether his results would be different if he wrote a letter that was nakedly honest. So he sat down and wrote the brazen truth about his strengths and weaknesses.

"I know how to program in Java," he said in one letter, referring to a computer program that was required for the job. "By that I mean I've used the program several times before, but like everyone else I will go look in a book when I'm asked to use it." He also wrote that he had been trained at a specific university, but then he added, "Truth is, I took a class once at that university and then I dropped out. But I'm pretty sure you won't check." He referred to himself as a "team leader," which he qualified by saying, "In other words, my boss likes me enough that if you call him he will say I am a 'team leader.' "

No one responded to his letter. "That's no worse than was the case before," he quickly points out.

Soon, he began writing all of his letters with self-defeating frankness. And as his phone remained silent, he grew more surprised by the lack of reaction. "I was applying to all these places that said they valued creativity," he says. "But then when creativity hit them in the face, they didn't even know it." He did not expect to get hired, but he did expect that at least one person in the several hundred human-resources offices he contacted would drop him a note simply saying thanks for the clever humor. It never happened.

In frustration, he shifted his approach, moving from candor to absurdity.

Previously he had been sending his real resume. He replaced it with a sheet of paper with "RESUME" underlined at the top and the words "Hire Me," and nothing else, in seventy-two-point lettering in the center of the page.

His cover letters featured a wry sense of humor. In one letter he explained that his prior job with Ford Motors involved leading the programming team in charge of assembly-line robotics. "My experience there taught me about the maximum speed and force with which you could have the robot insert a new part, without damaging the chassis of the vehicle," he wrote. "I feel that this experience will translate almost seamlessly to Transplantation Services at your hospital, and I think you will agree."

If anyone was laughing, they weren't telling Joey Comeau.

But one day he finally struck a chord, in a letter for a job opening at a bookstore. Having opened with the standard formalities about his sales experience and ability to work flexible hours, he wrote, "Should you require further information, or additional references, please do not hesitate to call. Also, do not hesitate to call if you are curious as to who would win in a fight between Ernest Hemingway and Morley Callaghan."

It continued: "Callaghan did win, during a friendly match where F. Scott Fitzgerald kept time. He did not keep it very well, and the winning blow was struck after the time had gone over, leading Hemingway to accuse F. Scott of rigging the match. A ridiculous literary feud followed, along with some pretty good books by all involved."

Comeau says he is still not sure why the bookstore hired him.

"I don't know," he said, "I guess they were looking for someone that customers would enjoy talking to but who also knew something about books."

THE CELL PHONE PRISON

One of the only things more tedious than a cutesy ring tone is a person who leaves his cell phone at his desk so that no one is there to answer it when he leaves.

Patti Beadles's office no longer has this problem.

Originally, unattended cell phones were especially annoying for Beadles and her colleagues, because all twenty-five people were crammed into one big room.

"Noise really carried," says Beadles, a forty-year-old executive from a small dot-com start-up in San Francisco.

Thus was born The Cell Phone Prison—a styrofoam cooler prominently displayed with a sign on top. Whenever someone leaves his phone at his desk and it begins ringing, it is the responsibility of the nearest person to fetch the cooler and place the phone inside, which muffles the sound to tolerable levels.

"People are usually so chagrined that they've been tossed into prison that they remember to take the phone with them next time," says Beadles, who invented the makeshift remedy. "I just wish there was a three-strikes law because most of our marketing department would be locked up permanently by now."

THE REJECTION REJECTION LETTER

Being unemployed is demoralizing. Selling yourself to try to get hired is alienating. Worst of all is getting turned down for the job, especially since the rejection letters are so cold and impersonal.

John Kador thought of something to send back.

Dear _____,
Thank you for your letter rejecting my application for employment with your firm.

I have received rejections from an unusually large number of well qualified organizations. With such a varied and promising spectrum of rejections from which to select, it is impossible for me to consider them all. After careful deliberation, then, and because a number of firms have found me more unsuitable, I regret to inform you that I am unable to accept your rejection.

Despite your company's outstanding qualifications and previous experience in rejecting applicants, I find that your rejection does not meet with my requirements at this time. As a result, I will be starting employment with your firm on the first of the month.

Circumstances change and one can never know when new demands for rejection arise. Accordingly, I will keep your letter on file in case my requirements for rejection change.

Please do not regard this letter as a criticism of your qualifications in attempting to refuse me employment. I wish you the best of luck in rejecting future candidates.

Sincerely,
John Kador

A writer of business and motivation books, Kador, fifty-four, says that he has been lucky enough not to have to use the letter himself. But countless people have asked to borrow it.

"Things have gotten so cold these days that many employers don't even send out a rejection letter," he says. "They just never get back to you."

BONE APPETIT

Some people see all property as public property. And when this type of person happens to work with you, it can become a problem.

Dena Roslan's colleague was especially fond of cookies. And since she was pregnant at the time and she regularly craved sweets, his sticky fingers were a frequent problem. To make matters worse, he was usually self-righteous about his thievery.

"It's about time you replenished your supply," Roslan remembers him saying once after she caught him red-handed.

Then one day she snapped. "I considered Ex-Lax brownies," she says. "But thinking of the consequences was too nasty."

So, on her way to work the next day, Roslan stopped off at Bone Giorno, a pet bakery near her home in Montville, New Jersey, and she bought a bag of dog biscuits that looked like biscotti.

"I laughed the whole way to my desk," recalls Roslan, who worked at the time as a clothing designer in New York City. "I could smell the biscuits and I knew they were going to taste gross."

Carefully setting the bait on her desk around lunchtime, she was sure to leave enticing crumbs strewn around her desk and one of the biscuits peeking invitingly from the bag.

Then she left the building for lunch. And sure enough, when she got back to her desk her colleague had finished off most of the bag.

"My only remorse was not being able to see his face after he ate the bait," she says.

4

❧

GOING POSTAL

There are two free AOL CDs in the mailbox and four catalogues advertising things you would never buy. The envelope with "Reply Required" printed on the front looks serious, and so does the $100 check made out to you inside, but it's just another marketing ploy. The stack of junk mail falls to the floor when you bend down to scrape up the three restaurant menus that were slipped under the door while you were at work.

Sometimes it feels like we are swimming upstream in a flood of stuff that we never asked to receive. We're so busy trying to keep the flow channeled to the trash can that there is hardly time left to put a stop to it.

But once in a while people devise some small ways to reverse the current or punish the source. And though the river keeps rising, these folks figure that they are not going under without a fight.

THE LONELINESS OF JUNK MAIL

At the end of the day, as we return home from work, there is a ritual that almost always brings with it a certain small dose of disappointment. We rifle through the stack of awaiting mail only to be shocked yet again at how little of it is actually worth reading. And how even less of it is actually directed at us, individually.

In the age of e-mail, we know not to expect personal letters. Bills, these days, are usually the most personalized thing to arrive in our mailboxes.

Nevertheless, there is still something that stings just slightly about the false hope buried among the real estate ads, grocery store circulars, and unsolicited catalogues. In addition to the wastefulness and aggressive commercialism of it all, there is a certain loneliness in the stacks of junk mail.

Matthew Roberts tries to make the best of it. He is excited when advertisement packets are sent to him not because he reads any of it, but because he uses the prepaid envelopes.

"They are quite valuable, really," says the twenty-three-year-old secretary at a pharmaceutical company in Corby, England. He keeps a stack of the envelopes in a neat pile on his counter alongside a blank sheet of envelope labels. When he needs to send a letter or bill, he overlays the original mailing address on the prepaid envelope with a blank sticker so that he can write in an address of his choice.

"It's an odd thing, I suppose, to be happy about getting junk mail," he said. "But I do like the free services they provide."

Roberts concedes that the tactic has become less effective in recent years as more response envelopes come with a bar code across the bottom that directs the envelope to a specific location.

"I'm just hoping they don't make a habit of using these bar codes," he said. "Or else I might have to go back to stamps."

Chris Marzuk points out that sometimes the junk mail is actually bundled with the bills themselves. "Every time I open my bill from MasterCard or Visa, there are at least a half dozen coupons or 'special order' forms for everything from cubic zirconia earrings to extension ladders," says Marzuk, a fifty-four-year-old school administrator from Greenlawn, New York. His habit is to fold these items up and put them in the return envelope with his statement and check. "The credit card companies should have to sort through the papers the same way I do," he says.

Laura Taalman takes a more cerebral approach. She likes to know how the junk-mail sender got her information. So when catalogues and other unsolicited items show up in her mailbox, she takes a close look at the spelling of her name, which tells her where the direct mail company bought her name.

The tactic works because every time she signs up for a new subscription to a magazine or gives money to a political group, she asks them whether they intend to sell her information. Invariably they say no. But as an added precaution she alters the spelling of her last name just slightly each time so that if the group or company does sell her information she will be able to find the culprit.

If it's Taalmen, she knows it was the Nature Conservancy that sold her details. If it's Telman, she knows it was *Harper's Magazine*.

"Eventually it gets hard to keep track of the slight variations," said Ms. Taalman, a thirty-two-year-old math professor at James Madison University in Virginia. "If I had been smart when I started doing this I would have used my cats' names or perhaps something like Taalwoman so that everything would be more obvious." Still, figuring out who gave up the goods on her provides just a little more sense of control over the flood that comes her way.

For some people that is not enough. For them, the point is to make the junk mailer pay a price. Wesley A. Williams spent more than a year pursuing this goal.

When signing up for a no-junk-mail list failed to stem the flow, he resorted to writing at the top of each unwanted item: "Not at this address. Return to sender." But the mail kept coming because the envelopes had "or current resident" on them, obligating mail carriers to deliver it.

Next, he began stuffing the mail back into the business reply envelope and sending it back so that the mailer would have to pay the postage.

"That wasn't exacting a heavy enough cost from them for bothering me," says Williams, a thirty-five-year-old middle school science teacher who lives in Melrose, New York, near Albany.

After checking with a postal clerk about the legality of stepping up his efforts, he began cutting up magazines, heavy bond paper, and small strips of sheet metal and stuffing them into the business reply envelopes that came with the junk packages.

"You wouldn't believe how heavy I got some of these envelopes to weigh," he says. "I was almost disappointed when the stuff stopped coming to my house."

"YOU'VE GOT MAIL!"

You don't need to look very far if you want to sign up for America Online. Their free CDs are about as ubiquitous as the air we breathe. But Jim McKenna can't get enough of them.

He used to hate receiving so many of these CDs. The wastefulness of sending them when most people just throw them away bothered him. One week, the volume of CDs was especially bad. The first three came in the mail. The fourth fell out of a magazine he was reading. The next three were packaged with computer hardware he bought. The final one was slipped into his bag when he went to his local video store.

"Eight AOL CDs in one week," recalls the thirty-seven-year-old Internet technology manager and Web developer, who lives in the San Francisco Bay Area. "And to think that I never even asked for one." So he decided he would send them back to AOL—once he collected a million of them.

As of May 2005, McKenna and his friend John Lieberman had collected 366,647 of the discs. When their collection reaches one million, they intend to rent an armada of trucks to deliver them back to AOL's headquarters.

"You've got mail!" he says. "That's exactly what I plan on saying to them."

McKenna admits that because of his job, he probably receives more of the CDs than most people. Nevertheless, he says, the problem is widespread. "We've got nothing against AOL as a company," he says. "We just think their marketing approach is extremely wasteful and can get on people's nerves."

McKenna says that AOL has never responded to his questions about how many CDs the company produces per year. He did, however, receive an e-mail several years ago from someone who claimed to have worked at a facility producing the CDs. That person said that the company was producing more than three hundred million of the discs per year. "And to think that these things take several hundred years to biodegrade when put in the landfill," McKenna says.

In August 2000, McKenna and Lieberman created a Web site about their campaign, and people immediately began donating their own CDs. Most of the collection is kept in Lieberman's backyard in forty-five plastic trash cans. McKenna says that each thirty-two-gallon can holds about five thousand CDs.

Donations have slowed recently, but McKenna still receives more than a hundred of the discs per month. He says that when they reach five hundred thousand, he and Lieberman will reassess whether they should make a road trip before reaching their goal. Estimating that a million CDs will weigh just over a ton, McKenna says that they may just rent a semi to haul them all. "I'm not sure what AOL will do when we get there," he says. "But really that's their concern, not ours."

THE UNBEARABLE LIGHTNESS
OF PENNYSAVERS

The only thing worse than junk mail delivered in your mailbox is when it's thrown in your front yard instead. While rushing out the door for work, the last thing anyone feels like doing is fishing unwanted solicitations out of the front hedges and walking back inside to throw them away. Yet, somehow, the weekly Pennysaver survives to this day as an institution of suburban living. These scrawny packets of advertisements and coupons bundled in clear plastic bags arrive with the regularity of the sun.

"Most people just leave it sitting there for days," says John Buck, a restaurant owner who lives in a split-level home on Long Island, New York.

But Buck prefers a tidier appearance, and four years ago he embarked on a losing battle against these unwanted savings packets. "They're nothing more than a bunch of classified ads for used cars, announcements for garage and yard sales, and a crossword puzzle that a deaf, dumb, and blind chimpanzee could finish in two minutes," he says. "They are tossed in my yard like legalized litter and I resent having to deal with it."

At least the people delivering them could toss them on the walkway or closer to the house so that the recipient does not have to go so far to fetch them, he says.

The easy solution was to contact the publisher, he figured. But every phone number he found led him to sales representatives for individual proprietors who use Pennysaver to advertise. So he turned to his local congressman. But the staffer on the phone seemed far more interested in fund-raising. Next he found that the Better Business Bureau couldn't care less. Neither did local environmental groups.

So Buck turned to the delivery people. "I've got nothing against them since they're just trying to get by," he says. "But I had nowhere else to turn." His plan was simple: Wait for the delivery. Run up to the car. Throw the Pennysaver back in the window.

"I had seen them once so I knew they drove this beat-up old wagon with a raspy muffler," he says. So he woke up early, perched on his porch and waited. And waited. And waited.

Finally, one weekend when his timing was right, he caught sight of the car, but it went by too quickly. "They are shooting for speed, not accuracy, as they roll by," he says. "So I couldn't get there fast enough and they were gone before I was even in motion."

Soon the delivery people fixed their muffler, cutting Buck's lead time significantly, and leaving him cursing and gesticulating as the car sputtered up the block. "I know I made too much of this but it was my obsession," he says, comparing himself to "a schizophrenic Bill Murray at war with a gopher."

But one day when all the variables fell in place, Buck made a strange discovery. He got to the curb in time to throw the Pennysaver back at the car, but it wouldn't fly. "They are pretty hard to toss, actually," he says. "They're just too light."

Demoralized, Buck gave up the effort to exact his small revenge. "I still find myself cursing as I head back inside," he says. "I can't help it, what can I say?"

HANDS OFF MY MAILBOX

Sometimes they are advertisements for handymen. Other times they offer gutter-cleaning services. Whatever their business, Bob Mitchell is not interested in anything that is sold with an advertisement stuck behind the red flag of his mailbox.

Like most people, he used to just throw them away. But the materials kept reappearing.

"They shouldn't just stick things wherever they please," says Mitchell, who is forty-four and runs a computer repair service in Bear, Delaware. "It's also illegal to tamper with a mailbox." So Mitchell printed a stack of special envelopes that he keeps at his desk for the occasion. Each envelope has the local postmaster's address already printed in the center. In the upper left-hand corner in the return address section each envelope says, "This item was illegally placed in my mailbox which is located at:" and then he includes his mailing address.

Mitchell says that he has talked to the postmaster, who told him that whenever his office receives such notices, it contacts the offender and issues a stern warning.

"I rarely see the same advertisement twice," Mitchell says. "I think that means that what I'm doing is working."

LITTER BETWEEN THE PAGES

They fall from between the pages of magazines with the aim of forcing us to notice them.

"They're actually designed to be annoying," says Andrew Kirk. "And I think generally they achieve that purpose."

Called "blow-in" cards, these small inserts are often subscription solicitations that are blown into the pages of magazines. They are stuck just firmly enough to remain in place until a reader opens to a certain page, which is when the cards flutter to the floor.

And in the process, they turn casual reading into a frustrating exercise in litter collection.

Kirk, a twenty-four-year-old freelance writer from Brooklyn, New York, often reads his magazines at his desk where he stacks the cards off to the side in an orderly pile. At the end of each month, he puts them in the mail but leaves them blank so that the advertiser is forced to pay the business reply postage without gaining a new subscriber.

"I help subsidize the post office," he says, "while also getting back at these advertisers at the same time."

Chris Marzuk takes a similar approach. But rather than leaving the cards blank, he fills them in with the address of the senders. "That way *Time* magazine can pay the return postage and also get plenty of subscriptions to *Time* magazine," says Marzuk, the school administrator from Greenlawn, New York, who also sends junk mail back to the credit card companies, with his payment. (See page 67.)

Sometimes the frustration with the cards is financial.

Kenn Fong, a fifty-year-old movie theater usher from Oakland, California, says that he once worked at a newsstand where the owner passed the time by pulling the cards out of all the magazines before displaying the magazines on the rack. At the end of the month he mailed them in blank.

"He was pissed off that the magazines were poaching his customers with subscriptions," Fong explains. "This was his little tactic for taking them on."

But occasionally, the cards actually have therapeutic purposes. "There is this saying that if you make a thousand origami cranes your wish will be granted," says Juliana Sadock Savino, fifty-one, a retired musician who lives just outside of Cleveland.

So, when her sister was ill and in the hospital, she collected the cards from the magazines in the waiting room and distracted herself during the long wait by making origami boxes out of them. The boxes were easier to make than cranes, she explains, adding that she still makes them at home and uses them for storage of her hairpins, paper clips, and earrings on her dresser.

"I don't know what you get if you make a thousand little boxes out of origami," she says. "Maybe you get a show in SoHo if they're good enough."

HOW TO WIN MAILBOX BASEBALL

Most people who live on a long straight road in a rural area have at least heard of mailbox baseball. Some of them have even been on the losing team.

Ray Hauser lives in a cul-de-sac. So he has never had the displeasure of finding his mailbox shattered into a thousand pieces and strewn about the neighbor's yard. He has, however, heard enough rantings from friends to know how angering it can be to deal with baseball bat–wielding hooligans who drive by late at night and get their jollies by knocking the tops off mailboxes.

"There was that famous scene in the movie *Stand by Me*," says Hauser, who is seventy-eight years old and lives in Boulder, Colorado. "I think that made mailbox baseball pretty famous."

Hauser is an inventor, so his inclination when he hears about a vexing problem is to try to design a solution. Several years after working on prototypes and testing them out with help from his grandchildren, he figured a way to level the playing field with mailbox batters.

The first device he built was called The Stinker. It features a pair of tubes that attach to the side of the mailbox, loaded with artificial skunk oil. When the mailbox is hit, the oil gets on the bat and spreads the scent into the culprit's car.

As a more aggressive approach, Hauser created The BatGrabber, which consists of a small hollow plastic tube with small nails inside. If a batter hits a mailbox with a wooden bat, which he said is the most common type of bat used, it gets stuck on the nails and is yanked from the batter's hands. "That can send quite a sting if the person is driving by fast," he says.

The third device offers the chance to get a license plate from the culprit. The Tattler is a small transmitter that wirelessly sends a signal to the house informing the owner of the mailbox that it has been opened or struck.

"These are mostly just kids trying to have fun," Hauser says. "My goal is to help them realize that this game might not be as much fun as they thought it would be."

WHEN CUSTOMERS DO THE DELIVERING

Every day when Ben Hoffstein returns to his apartment after a long day at work, he finds himself performing the same tedious ritual: he drops his bags, hangs his jacket, and heads back to pick up all the take-out menus that delivery people have slipped under his door.

"It's a total pain," says the twenty-nine-year-old broker at a Manhattan hedge fund. "I'm tired and the last thing I feel like doing is scraping these things off the floor."

Hoffstein used to complain to his wife about it, but this provided little consolation. Confronting delivery people in the hall and asking them to stop didn't get lasting results either. Then he thought of a way to turn the tables.

Once a week or so, he takes a stroll around his neighborhood. Visiting nearby restaurants, he takes a stack of the take-out menus that many of them keep in storage racks on the sidewalk near the front door. He then drops them off at whatever restaurant has "littered" under his door during the prior week.

"My wife gets pretty embarrassed when I do it," he says. "So I tend to make the most thorough rounds when she goes out of town."

The best approach, he says, is to pit two offending institutions against each other. That involves taking a thick stack of menus from one and dropping them off inside the doorway of the other, and vice versa.

"That way, one guy is losing printing costs," he says, "while the other one has to clean up the floor just like they're making me do at home."

5

❦

PRESS 1 FOR AGGRAVATION

If you don't hate loud cell phone talkers then you probably are one.

And while the rest of us bite our tongues hoping for your reception to fail, it is hard not to wonder whether Alexander Graham Bell had any idea what his invention would bring.

How would he have handled the telemarketer who calls during supper? Would he have pulled his hair out as the automated operator made him repeat his name a fourth time only to still get it wrong?

But in the right hands, the telephone can be used for good, which truly makes Bell's invention indeed a sword that cuts both ways.

It's anyone's guess.

SNEAKING OUT OF PURGATORY

They start with a discouraging forecast of how long the wait is going to be. Then come the repeated requests to visit them on the Web instead. After that, they chime in with the bad music. An obsequious voice interrupts every so often to remind: "Your call is important to us. Thank you for your continued patience."

Welcome to purgatory.

"I could pass three birthdays before someone would get on the line," says Peter Remler, a loan officer for a mortgage company based in Kingston, New York. "But I'd have to sit there like everyone else and stew while I waited."

Like many people, Remler hated calling to book airline tickets because the wait on hold was so agonizing.

But one day he had an idea: he noticed that at the beginning of the phone tree that started calls to the airline reservation line, the recording said that he could press 1 for English or 2 for another language.

"I only speak English and not enough Spanish to pull off booking a flight," Remler explains. "So I'd be in trouble if the operator answered in anything other than English." But the operator who picks up always speaks English, he says. And from their tone of voice, they seem happy to be put to work.

"I apologize for choosing the non-English option

and tell her that I couldn't get through on the other line," Remler says. "To this day, I've never been turned away."

Michael McLaughlin has an even craftier approach.

With many help lines, if a caller presses one number above what the menu gives as an option it gets the caller into a secret, advanced help line, he explains.

"Okay, it's not so secret," he says, "but it is the advanced help route that is usually reserved for privileged customers who have paid a lot of money to be able to avoid long waits on hold."

Having worked for the past three years at a call center in Princeton, New Jersey, McLaughlin says that he learned the trick by watching the way client companies typically set up their accounts. He said he also tests the tactic when he calls any place with a phone tree that says press 1 for this or press 2 for that.

"It has worked about twenty-five percent of the time," he says. "The rest of the time, I just put the phone on speaker and sit there and wait like everyone else."

MAKE THEM CHASE THEIR TAILS

The occasional wrong number is one thing. But when the mistake gets emblazoned on official stationery, the influx of misdirected calls can drive a person batty.

Aaron Westbrook was getting several hundred misdirected calls per month after a law practice in his neighborhood set up a new phone number that was almost identical to his. "It was nonstop," says Westbrook, thirty-four, who works in a rubber products factory in Princeton, Indiana. "Every time the phone rang I wondered if it was really for me."

After calling the law firm and asking them to find a phone number that wasn't so similar to his, he was told that they were not willing to make that change.

So he decided to make some changes of his own.

First, he changed his answering machine to redirect the misdialers to the law office's proper number. But the calls kept coming.

Then he tried a comical approach. He set his answering machine message to politely direct callers to his own number, the one they had just dialed. "It was incredible," he says. "People would actually call over and over and over again, never figuring out that they were in a loop."

After the joke finally wore old, Westbrook changed his machine again. This time he gave the law firm's correct number. But the recording also instructed callers to mention that they had heard this message, because if they did, they would be entitled to a lesser fee from their lawyer.

That seemed to get the job done. "The call volume diminished significantly after that," he says.

THE GRANDDADDY OF ALL ANNOYANCES

The last thing anyone wants is to get caught by a tele-marketer before sitting down to dinner. And with the creation of the national "Do Not Call" registry, a lot of the passive-aggressive creativity that people previously used to fend off these calls has been wasted. Neverthe-less, there are millions of people who have not signed up and many of them still employ their own tactics for dealing with the unsolicited calls.

Jason Eshleman uses one of the most popular methods. He asks the caller to hold on for a minute and then he leaves the person waiting indefinitely. "This slows down the time between calls," says Eshleman, a thirty-three-year-old anthropologist living in Berkeley, California. "The industry depends on reaching a large number of people since the return on sales is very low."

Steve Teller uses the same trick, but with a twist. He only pretends to put the person on hold but instead places them on speakerphone. When the telemarketer begins pleading: "Hello, can you hear me? Is anyone there?" Teller pretends that he can't hear them and he keeps typing on his computer.

"I've had some remain on the phone for fifteen minutes," says Teller, who is thirty-seven and lives in western Canada. Teller says that sometimes he and his wife have conversations near the phone for added effect, asking each other, "Honey can you hear that? What is that noise?" as the waiting telemarketer pleads for their attention.

David Neiblum's secret weapon is his three-year-old daughter.

"The first time we used this tactic was when a telemarketer asked for the lady of the house and I handed the phone to Anna, the chattiest of our twins," said Neiblum, a forty-two-year-old gastroenterologist who lives in West Chester, Pennsylvania. "She started telling the hapless marketer about her Elmo doll until they eventually hung up."

Since he works for a phone system company, Garry Polmateer has special features on the phones in his home. When telemarketers call he puts them on hold and pipes in annoying music and a specially created recording. "Please hold the line," it says in the standard voice. "Your call is very unimportant to us."

But some people, including Jason Catlett, would rather be effective than humorous when it comes to dealing with telemarketers. Catlett has created a high-stakes quiz to use against telemarketers. If the telemarketers refuse to answer or they give the wrong answer to any of the questions on the quiz, the recipient of the call has grounds to sue, he explains. Here are some of the questions:

- "Could you tell me your full name please?"
- "And a phone number, area code first?"
- "What's the name of the organization you're calling for?"
- "Does that organization keep a list of numbers it's been asked not to call?"
- "I would like my number(s) put on that list. Can you take care of that now?"
- "Will your company keep my info on its no-call list for at least ten years?"
- "And does your company have a written policy that says that on paper?"
- "Can you send me a copy of it?"

And on and on the list goes.

Catlett, who has posted the list at a Web site he created called junkbusters.com, said that he compiled it after moving in 1992 from Sydney, Australia, to New Jersey to take a job working in AT&T's research laboratory. "I hooked up my phone and the very first call I received was from someone trying to sell me something," he says. Having studied the problem while working for AT&T, he became something of an expert on the legalities of telemarketing.

"I don't know how many people in total have sued, though I know there are a handful," he says. "But usually the script is enough to get the calls to stop."

IT WORKS BOTH WAYS

Like everyone else, telemarketers have peeves, too. Topping their list are the ornery people who throw tantrums about unsolicited calls.

"Within a week of doing that job you've seen it all before," says Dan Mallon, who worked in 2000 as a telemarketer in Ramsey, New Jersey, while in high school. "For us, it was the people who flip out and the people who think they are actually fooling you that were the most tedious."

So telemarketers have devised their own ways of fighting back.

Mallon, who now works for a publishing company in the Bronx, says that during the year or so that he worked for the telemarketing company, he and his co-workers kept a special list. If a person screamed and demanded that the telemarketers never call again, they added that person's name and phone number to the list. If a person put the telemarketer on hold indefinitely, their name also went on the list. "By far the most common one we heard was, 'Give me your number and I'll call you back during dinner,'" he says. "We definitely got back at them."

The fate of the people on the special list varied. During slow times, Mallon and his friends would pull names from the list to make crank calls pretending that he was calling from the zoo about an escaped animal in their neighborhood. Other times, they simply reshuffled the numbers on the special list back into the database so that those people would be sure to get more calls during the next call cycle. "Some nights we did nothing but make crank calls and go after these people," he says.

For quality control, the telemarketing company recorded most of the calls but no one ever actually listened to the recordings, Mallon says. He also observed that because the commissions were so minimal, most people were there simply to clock hours.

These days, Mallon says, revenge would be more difficult because telemarketing firms rely on computers to do the dialing so that the callers don't know the number of the person they are calling.

"Still, I'm sure they've found some new ways to get at these people," he says. "I'm just glad I'm not doing it anymore."

"CAN YOU HEAR ME NOW?"

When it comes to public spaces, silence is part of what belongs to the public. But increasingly, cell phone talkers commandeer this shared good and fill it with their own idle chatter.

Sometimes their babble is painful for its sheer banality. Other times they delve into topics that to discuss out loud would make even the most intimate of friends blush.

But these people, in all of their loud self-importance, don't seem to notice. Or at least they don't seem to care.

The Web offers a booming trade in pocket-sized jammers, which block cell phone signals within a forty-five-foot radius. Unfortunately, the devices are illegal to use in the United States, so law abiders, left to fend for themselves, tend to resort to lower-tech guerrilla tactics.

Rich Hilbert says that he most often encounters loud cell phone talkers in airports. His tactic is to hold up the small tape recorder that he keeps with him, as if to record the loud talker. "They go into that hand-over-mouthpiece mode," says Hilbert, a fifty-seven-year-old sociology professor at Gustavus Adolphus College in St. Peter, Minnesota. "Occasionally someone will complain that I am violating some kind of agreement or something, but it certainly isn't something I agreed to."

Susan Lulic reads aloud when confronted with this situation. "Last time I read several articles from *The New York Times Magazine* and *Nature Conservancy*," says Lulic, the educator from Tucson, Arizona, who also offered a creative solution to cope with inconsiderate dog walkers. (See page 8.) "Usually the person on the phone gets really ticked off and the other people sitting nearby throw me appreciative glances."

But if the conversation veers toward the raunchy— and amazingly enough it often does—those within earshot are usually left with no other option than to vacate the area. "You hardly want to hear everything about what happened at the end of that person's date last night," says Jim Coudal, forty-five, who owns a design firm in Chicago. "Then that person hangs up and calls three more people, telling it again and again in even more graphic detail." The indignant stare rarely works with these people, and interrupting the conversation usually seems like more effort than it's worth, he says.

That's why "Dear Cell Phone User" cards come in handy. Produced by the Society for Handheld Hushing—or SHHH!—a fake group that Coudal invented, the cards read as follows:

Dear Cell Phone User:
We are aware that your ongoing conversation about
_____ is very important to you, but we thought
that you'd like to know that it doesn't interest us in the
least. In fact, your babbling disregard for others is
more than just a little annoying.

Since they are fill-in-the-blank, the cards can be tailored to fit the occasion. For instance, the card on Coudal's Web site has *"your husband's vasectomy"* written into the blank. In the last year, more than three hundred thousand people have downloaded the wallet-sized cards, which are free online.

Coudal believes that loud cell phone talkers are practically a universal frustration these days. He points out that French, Swedish, and Japanese versions of the cards have already appeared online. "Everyone wants a way to tell the obnoxious cell phone user that they are being a pain," he says. "But they want to do it discreetly."

PUTTING DIRECTORY ASSISTANCE
IN SLOW MOTION

"Wait," you say, "I also need the address." But it's too late. The automated voice is already reciting the phone number and the live operator has hurried on to the next call.

Sometimes, dialing directory assistance can feel like a speed sport.

There is a fleeting moment, wedged tightly between the first automated operator, who asks, "What listing?" and who rarely understands what you say, and the second automated operator, who methodically recites the phone number. Move too slowly and the short-lived chance to talk to a human being disappears, and you're looking at another $1.50 to call back.

"Plus, one out of three times you are given the wrong number or the automated operator says that there is no listing for something like Citibank or American Airlines," says Chris Fiore, a fifty-eight-year-old retail executive for a large clothing company based in New York. "So you have to pay twice for their mistake."

Contesting the charge seems petty and not worth the effort. "Are you really going to explain that you shouldn't be charged $1.50 because you needed a second to think?" Fiore says.

Instead, he takes a slightly deceptive approach. "I rarely need two numbers but I usually say I do," he says. Like many people, he circumvents the first computerized agent by simply saying "operator" over and over again until the computer hands him over to a human being. Then he says he wants two listings, which is the amount that callers are usually entitled to request per call to directory assistance.

After the operator gives him the information for his first listing, he thinks for a moment or two about whether he has all the information he wants, and he then says, "Oh, I'm sorry, that's all I need." Since two calls to 411 rarely connect to the same operator, no one seems to notice his tactic, he says.

"It puts things on your terms," Fiore says. "At $1.50 for thirty seconds worth of help, I think that's only fair."

TREAT ME LIKE I'M CRAZY AND
I'LL ACT LIKE IT

Sometimes when you call to report a problem, customer service representatives treat you as though the problem is a figment of your imagination. Tom Mabe decided to play the part.

All he wanted to do was cancel his cell phone account. But the cell phone company told him he would be penalized more than $100 if he did. So he decided to wait for the contract to expire. Suddenly and inexplicably, he was changed to a new calling plan without notification. When he called to complain, the representative from the cell phone company said he would correct the problem, but instead he renewed Mabe's two-year contract, extending the amount of time he would have to stay with the company.

That's when the echoes started.

"Every time I made a call there were two of me on the line," says Mabe, a thirty-seven-year-old stand-up comedian from Louisville, Kentucky. "I thought I was going crazy."

When he called customer service to deal with his new problem, the representative said she could not hear an echo. "She copped the biggest attitude," he says. "It was like I had interrupted her during dinner or something."

Several additional calls to the customer service line met with the same response. So Mabe decided to make sure the operator could hear the echo. He called back, but this time he had a friend with a much deeper voice on the line as well.

"Everything I said, he repeated a couple seconds later," Mabe recounts, explaining that he acted indignant when the representative accused him of playing a prank. "At least she didn't say that she didn't hear anything else on the line."

WHY SHOULD THEY BE THE ONLY ONES RECORDING OUR CONVERSATIONS?

Few things are as frustrating as talking to an unmotivated customer service representative when you need help fast. For David Hume it was a matter of life and death.

In the fall of 2003, while driving along on a desert road in Namibia, Hume and his girlfriend, Lisa Sanguedolce, hit a rut and flipped their car. Sanguedolce broke her neck and was rushed to the hospital. Hume needed to get clearance from the health insurance company for doctors to perform a certain medical procedure, but he was placed on hold for almost an hour. Then he was passed among several operators, none of whom had a clue how to answer his simple question. "No one seemed to recognize the urgency of the situation," he says.

After his call was disconnected because his calling card ran out of minutes, he called back and was told that there was no record of the prior conversation having happened. So he had to start the whole process over again from scratch.

"I've never been so mad in my life," says Hume, a twenty-nine-year-old former investment banker who now lives in London.

Eventually his girlfriend was treated. With time,

she healed. But Hume stayed mad. "I couldn't do anything afterwards because I had no record of what happened on the phone," he says. "In cases like this, it doesn't make sense that the company is the only one with a recording."

So Hume created Registered Call, a company that offers a central phone number where people can call and have phone conversations recorded. By dialing the number, people are connected with an automated operator that directs the call to whatever number is requested. For legal reasons, the system states that the call is being recorded for quality purposes. "It's amazing how effective it is to turn the tables," Hume says. "If things don't go well, all the customer has to do is pull the recorded conversation down from their account on our Web site and e-mail the CEO of the company."

6

VEHICULAR MISANTHROPY

As if tolls, long commutes, congestion, and pot-holes weren't enough. We also have one another.

Maybe too much time trapped in our little metal boxes breeds contempt for our fellow travelers. But in a perfect world no one else would use the roads and we would park our cars in lots that were always empty.

Unfortunately, that is not our world. So as we drive around looking for a parking spot because some idiot took up two spaces, we have little alternative but to stew in our own road rage. As we are blinded by that tailgater in the SUV whose headlights shine directly at eye level in our rearview mirror, all we can do is curse to the silence of our cars.

Au contraire.

Consider the true road warriors. They are the ones who do something else.

GUERRILLA WARFARE IN THE PARKING LOT

It's difficult to say which is worse: a bad parker or a greedy one. Either way, both use up space that doesn't belong to them and both test the limits of our patience.

Chris Myers is thankful that he grew up next to a parking lot. His favorite childhood prank is serving him well in dealing with these types of annoying people.

Whenever someone parks in a space reserved for the disabled, he leaves a note on the windshield that says, "I'm so sorry I hit your car. It doesn't look like the damage was severe." Then he signs a name but he makes it just messy enough to be illegible.

"It works best if the person owns a fancy car," says the thirty-one-year-old student at the University of Wisconsin at Madison. "The driver scrambles around trying to find the damage, and then they're also faced with the decision of whether to call and report it to the police even though they are parked in an illegal space."

And if he is feeling particularly perverse, Myers adds a phone number to the note.

"The best is to use a phone number for a group that advocates on behalf of the disabled," he says.

Jason J. Brunet has created a flyer for those who can not seem to limit themselves to one parking space.

"Free Parking Tutorial!" it says, with a small picture showing a car that is properly centered in its parking space. "Learn Parking in One Easy Lesson!" At the bottom, the flyer provides a Web address that Brunet has set up, where visitors are offered various bird's-eye diagrams showing what good and bad parking jobs look like.

"It's odd," says Brunet, a twenty-four-year-old student at a technical college in New Orleans. "I designed this with the full expectation that I would get hate mail, but I haven't gotten any even though there is lots of traffic on the Web site."

Perhaps the reason is that sometimes the bad parking jobs are intentional.

Worried about getting door dings, these drivers tend to put their prized vehicles in the far reaches of a parking lot, where no one else is around, angling them so that others will be less inclined to park alongside.

David Coe goes the distance to irritate these people.

Even if there is a parking space closer, Coe drives his old Subaru wagon out to that spacious corner and pulls it up right next to the expensive vehicle. "I make sure it's just within ding distance," says Coe, thirty-three, who owns a small knitting shop in Flagstaff, Arizona.

What bothers him, he says, is the sense of entitlement of the other driver in presuming that it is all right to take several parking spaces. "They also clearly take their car a little too seriously," he says. "So I make sure that guy knows that for every one of them, there is a guy like me."

Steve Durfee is one of "them."

After owning "old junkers" for most of his life, Durfee splurged and bought himself a racing-green BMW Mini Cooper. "She's my baby," says the fifty-three-year-old pharmaceutical company executive, who lives in Salt Lake City. But within a week of owning the car, he says, someone hit it with a shopping cart.

So Durfee now makes a habit of parking it far away from everyone else. "I'd love to put it diagonally across two spaces so no one can come near," he says. "But it's so darn small that it wouldn't do any good because it won't take up the space."

Often when Durfee leaves his car safe and removed, he returns to find someone who has parked next to him anyway even though there are other spots that are equally convenient. "I don't see their point," he says, explaining that he retaliates by poking the person's side-view mirror so that the driver will have to readjust it when using the car the next time.

"I make sure it's all out of whack and facing the sky," he says. "Maybe, just maybe, that person will think twice the next time they decide to park next to someone who clearly doesn't want any cars near them."

SINCE SLAMMING ON THE BRAKES
IS NOT AN OPTION

No amount of speed satisfies some drivers. They barrel down on whatever car is in front of them, bullying anyone who gets in their way.

But tailgaters often drive spiffy cars, which is why Allan Doeksen's defense tactic works so well.

Doeksen hates when people drive too close. "I'm definitely not a slowpoke," he says. "In the city, I go the speed limit, and outside the city I go way above."

Still, there is always someone who wants to push the limits. And that person often ends up behind Doeksen. So he decided to make a small adjustment to his Jeep Cherokee to get his point across. He adjusted the nozzles on his rear windshield wiper so that instead of spraying his back window, they now spray the fluid at the car behind him.

"It's a little tinkle to show them what I think," says Doeksen, whose "road rage" also shows up at the supermarket. (See page 44.)

Rather than hitting the tailgater's windshield, the nozzle spray hits the hood of the tailgating car, which is a less dangerous tactic, he explains: "Let's just say that the windshield wiper fluid doesn't do great things to the paint job if it's left there too long."

Steve Kline likes to aim a little higher when targeting tailgaters. He tries to play mind games by flipping on his turn signal and varying his driving speed gently. The tailgaters usually drop back out of nervousness that he will suddenly slow down to make his turn.

"There is nothing that drives me nuts more than when people leave their turn signal blinking and they don't turn," says Kline, who is twenty-three and a video game tester for a software company in Springfield, Illinois. "The only thing worse is probably someone who tailgates."

Brian Stucki has taken this frustration to the next level.

Back in college, Stucki and his friends at Brigham Young University thought they might try picking up girls by installing a small scrolling screen on the back of Stucki's Chevy pickup truck. "You'd be amazed at how well the thing worked," he says.

Positioned just above the truck's "Chevy" lettering, the two-by-sixteen-inch screen is attached to the pull-down flap on the back of the flatbed. The scrolling screen, which is protected from the elements by a small lip, is wired to a small laptop computer sitting inside the center console of the truck, where Stucki or his passenger can type a message for display.

When an attractive driver cruised by, Stucki would usually instruct whoever was riding copilot to prepare a message. "First, we'd throw a friendly wave and a smile as we passed," says Stucki, who is twenty-five years old and an Apple computer salesman who lives in Las Vegas. "Then once we were in front we'd say, 'Hey, here's our cell number. Give us a quick call.' " Since they were in a college town, people were unusually friendly, and girls were almost always so amused that they called right away.

His dating days are over. But Stucki says he uses his scrolling screen now more than ever. "These days it's all tailgaters and cell phone talkers," he says.

Stucki adds that he is careful not to say anything that will spark road rage. For tailgaters, he usually writes: "We can just latch you to my hitch if you're going to ride that close." For cell phone talkers, he often uses: "Hang up your phone! You're risking my life."

He also concedes that the notes he broadcasts often only give the cell phone talkers something to talk about. "Still," he says, "once in a while they get the message."

THE PARKING METER FAIRIES

If life in the big city is measured in seconds, then parking in the big city is measured in fractions of a second. While most city slickers have it down to a science when it comes to beating the clock and feeding parking meters on time, there are few things that can ruin a day faster than sprinting back to a meter and arriving barely ten seconds late to find a ticket already waiting.

"It was incredible how zealous the parking Gestapo used to be around here," says Susan Pacillo, who lives in Anchorage, Alaska. "It was one guy who would slink around the corner and when your meter was within range of expiring he would start writing the ticket so that he could put it on your car the moment the red flag went up."

This was an especially vexing problem for Pacillo, a forty-seven-year-old domestic-violence counselor in downtown Anchorage. Several of her clients stopped coming to meet with her because they said they could not afford risking another parking fine.

So she devised her own solution: she kept a jar of pocket change on her desk and every two hours she took it with her on a stroll up the block to feed the meters at each of her clients' cars. But one day she noticed an expression of annoyance on the parking officer's face as she passed him, and she realized that her actions were getting to him.

Pacillo then decided to feed the meters of all the cars on the block that were near the time limit. "It was just a couple of dimes in each meter," she says. "But boy did it piss him off."

Pacillo's irritation with the parking authority only grew when she received a ticket on her sister's truck for an expired sticker. After failing to get the ticket dropped, Pacillo convinced her sister, Linny, to start a competition at a gas station they owned in town.

Placing a collection jar on the counter near the register, the sisters solicited donations to the "parking fairies" who would begin randomly feeding meters downtown for the sake of randomly spreading kindness to parkers and frustration to the enforcement authorities.

The reaction was overwhelming. "The jar overflowed on the first day," Pacillo says. "We had to put out a second one." Since the money was coming in faster than they could use it to feed meters, the sisters decided to use some of it to buy costumes befitting parking fairies—pink tutus, blue leotards, and long underwear. They also bought a small go-cart from a local junk dealer, which they christened the "parking fairy mobile." The vehicle featured a line on the front hood from an Aaron Tippin song: "You Gotta Stand for Something or You'll Fall for Anything."

"This was July 1994," Pacillo recalls. "Our intention was to do it for a couple weekends that summer." But three years later, the fairies were still at it, spending an average of twenty hours per week delivering last-minute reprieves a nickel at a time.

"We became minor folk heroes," says Pacillo. But they weren't so minor.

In 1997, Anchorage city officials passed Proposition 3, which extended the amount of time people could remain in parking spaces and transferred the responsibility of monitoring the meters from independent hands to the local police department. The parking meter fairies, clad in tutus and all, testified on behalf of the measure. Soon thereafter, the city also gave the fairies an award in recognition for their work. "The award said that in our small gestures we had reminded the state and city that government is still by the people and for the people," says Pacillo. "We decided at that point that it was safe to burn our wings."

STUTTERING AT STOP SIGNS

Manners make the world a kinder and gentler place. They also slow down traffic and confuse the rules of the road.

Missy Kaberline confronts this reality every time she rolls up to a stop sign. "When a driver arrives to a four-way stop sign they are supposed to yield to the person on the right," she says. "If you're the driver on the right, then move your damn car!"

Sometimes distracted cell phone talkers are the culprits. But far more often, she says, polite people are the ones to initiate an ungraceful dance that can only be called stop-sign stuttering.

It goes like this: you roll up to a stop sign at the same moment as another driver to your right. You then wave the other driver on, who waves the same gesture back to you. Both of you stare blankly at each other. No one knows who should move. Just as you start to inch forward, the other driver starts proceeding as well. You both slam on your brakes.

"The rules are pretty clear," says Kaberline, a twenty-nine-year-old accounts manager for a graphics company in Spokane, Washington. "So there is really no reason for this to happen."

Kaberline avoids it all by making a habit of declining all offers of kindness when they come at a stop sign.

If it is not her turn to go, she sits and motions until the polite driver does what he is supposed to do. "I don't care if they wave me on," she says. "I just stay there no matter what."

WHEN BUMPERS BECOME PULPITS

Even driving has become a chance for some people to profess their faith. "God Is My Co-Pilot" and "Jesus Saves" bumper stickers seem to call out at virtually every other stoplight.

Jim Walker found a way to answer back.

"I don't see why people feel the need to use the bumper of their car to push their beliefs," says the fifty-six-year-old mechanical engineer, who lives in Miami.

As an atheist, Walker says that he has his own views about religion. But he also says that he has never considered sharing these views indiscriminately with everyone who pulls up behind his car. "I just find the whole instinct bizarre," he says.

So one day he thought of an idea while waiting at a stoplight. In his rearview mirror he could see the word "ambulance" written with inverted lettering on the hood of the emergency vehicle stopped behind him. When Walker returned home he used his computer to create several small antireligious signs written in the same inverse lettering that he had seen on the ambulance. Attaching the signs using Velcro to the back of his rearview mirror, he was able to display his message directly within the sight of the driver in front of him.

"It was great because it gets the message across

directly to the person you are targeting and no one else," he says.

Now, when he is stuck behind a driver with the Christian fish attached to the back, Walker reaches for the card with the image of a large fish eating a smaller one and the word "Reality" written across the middle.

And when confronted by the "Don't Follow Me, Follow Jesus" bumper sticker, Walker reaches for his "God Is Myth" card.

"I figure that if they are going to get preachy with me," he says, "then I should respond."

MAKE YOURSELF THE DELIVERY

Anyone who has lived in a big city has experienced the frustration of driving around endlessly looking for a parking space. Todd Lappin hasn't had to deal with this annoyance in a long time.

He lives in San Francisco and drives an SUV. But he never struggles to find parking because even though he is forbidden, he always leaves his vehicle in the loading zones downtown or along the yellow curb reserved for delivery trucks.

He gets away with it because he invented Telstar Logistics, a fake company whose name he has put on official-looking stickers that he attached to his truck. His "urban camouflage," as he calls it, also includes a yellow and black striped sticker that runs just above his back bumper that gives the feel of a utility truck. On the side windows, the truck features the company logo: an aeronautical symbol with a subtitle that reads: "Land, Air, Sea, Space." Several times a month, he parks exactly where he wants and only occasionally gets a ticket, he says.

"I'm careful not to break the law," says Lappin, explaining that whenever he is asked by a law enforcement officer about the truck, he always says that it is a fake company that he created.

Lappin thought up the idea while he was an undergraduate at Brown University. He and his housemate at the time, Wayne, invented TNW Industries (the abbreviation roughly stood for Todd and Wayne), and they decked their two vehicles with official-looking company stickers that they printed on their home computers. With the dot-com boom, Lappin figured it was time to adopt a more technical-sounding company name. So he came up with Telstar Logistics.

"It's all about strategic ambiguity when you choose the company name," says Lappin, who is thirty-seven years old and a magazine editor. When people ask him about his vehicle, he tells them that it's a company that does "integrated services." "People usually just walk away looking puzzled like they should know what that means," he says.

Lappin says he was recently surprised to find out that there is an actual company with the name Telstar. "Well," he says, "I think I'm going to have to have my legal department talk to their lawyers."

7

❦

RAGE AGAINST THE MACHINE

The first e-mail was a quick "hi" from a friend, but at the bottom it had nine lines of legal mumbo jumbo warning of what would happen if anyone else read the note. The next e-mail was yet another chain letter, this one threatening twenty years of bad luck for not forwarding it. Then came three advertisements for penis extensions and a letter from a man in Africa pleading for help with an embezzlement scheme.

Sometimes checking your e-mail can feel like a jaunt through the Twilight Zone. Perhaps the anonymity of the Web lowers inhibitions a bit too far.

But the medium is also subject to the laws of physics. And for every annoying and idiotic action there is an equal and opposite reaction. For that, we should all be thankful.

URGENT AND CONFIDENTIAL

They are as desperate as they are formulaic. And with the spread of the Internet, the so-called "Nigerian letters" have grown from being an occasional curiosity to a relentless plague on our in-boxes.

Under a subject line that reads "Urgent and Confidential," these scams usually open with, "I am in search of a reputable person to assist me with an urgent business matter." And they go on to explain that some important government official has died and that there is a need to remove a large amount of money from the country before other officials seize it.

"Any help you provide in the effort," the e-mail usually says, "will be repaid with a large percentage of the money." And while the ubiquity of these scam e-mails should undermine their effectiveness, somehow they persist.

In 1996, Lee Kennedy was receiving an average of four or five of the letters by fax and e-mail per day. "What got to me about them was the sheer quantity," says Kennedy, who is fifty-one years old and a food chemist for a large company based in Melbourne, Australia. "They're also amazingly foolish and blatant scams."

So one day Kennedy decided to reply.

Using an alias, he wrote that he wanted to learn

more about the business offer. And with that, he began a ten-year habit of scamming the scammers as he wove elaborate webs—often cast with characters drawn from history or famous works of fiction—looping the scammers into drawn-out correspondences that sometimes lasted up to a year.

"These scams are ridiculous," he says. "But they've definitely provided me with quite a bit of fun."

For every half-baked explanation a scammer sent about the origin of the money, Kennedy included an implausible feature to his own story. With each fake tax form or faux lawyer's bill that the scammer sent to justify the need for small amounts of money, Kennedy replied with a fake newspaper profile or an official-looking travel itinerary to bolster his own responses.

Before long, Kennedy found himself juggling multiple stories at once, spending close to twenty-five hours a week keeping the scammers looped in. "I'm much more efficient now since I have a lot of the documents on file," he says. "Still, creating new stories takes a fair amount of work."

But none compare to his masterpiece about Don Quixote. "I think that was definitely my best work," Kennedy says.

After being contacted by an African scammer calling himself Nelson Kalu, Kennedy responded as Don Quixote. "I do not know if I can help you but I do take pride in supporting worthy quests," Mr. Quixote wrote. "I am a country gentleman, no longer young."

Always sprinkled with direct passages from Cervantes's classic work, the communications quickly culminated in Kalu's request that Mr. Quixote come to visit him in Benin to finalize the deal.

Mr. Quixote agreed to the request. But first he explained that he would need to travel with two others. "My party would include my faithful servant, Sancho Panza, and my Lady Dulcinea," he wrote.

All are welcome, Kula responded.

Next, Mr. Quixote wrote that there was a problem with the flight: Air France said that he could not bring his horse on board.

"If Air France does not want to carry your horse, don't worry," Kula replied. "I am going to make arrangements to hire one for you in Cotonou."

Many letters and much planning later, the two men finally spoke on the phone. Kula mentioned that Mr. Quixote sounded young for his age. Never passing up an opportunity to press the limits of credulity, Mr. Quixote replied that, in fact, he looked even younger than he sounded because he had received plastic surgery. "I owe all my looks to Dr. Polly Urethane, a plastic surgeon at St. John's Hospital in Sydney," he said.

Finally, after sending Kula their official travel itinerary, Mr. Quixote and his entourage set out on their journey.

Unfortunately, Mr. Quixote ran into problems after he lost his temper in Paris.

"French See Red over Attack on Moulin Rouge" was the headline that ran in the *Cockie Cage Liner*, which Mr. Quixote's lawyer sent to Kula to explain what happened. The article said that three Australian tourists had stolen horses from Parisian police officers and charged the famous theater, ominously waving baguettes. After being arrested, the three were later released. Eventually, the lawyer said, Mr. Quixote and his group got back on their way. They flew to Cairo, where they were to proceed overland to Benin.

That's when the real tragedy struck.

"It is with a heavy heart that I must convey to you the melancholy news that Mr. Don Quixote has been found dead in the north Sahara," read the next e-mail that came from Mr. Quixote's lawyer. Attached was a newspaper article—which like all of Kennedy's handi-work was impressively realistic—that explained that Mr. Quixote had been attacked by a pack of about forty men led by a man named Ali Baba.

Kennedy says that although he has been spinning ridiculous yarns for years in correspondences with scammers, few people ever seem to catch on.

"Considering that they are scam artists them-selves, it's incredible how thick some of these people are," says Kennedy, who has posted his many epistolary exchanges with the scammers on his Web site, sweetchillisauce.com. "The only time I've been snagged by a reference was a lady who realized that the picture I sent of myself was actually of our prime minister, John Howard."

Kennedy says that he has received half a dozen e-mails over the years from people who actually lost money in these scams. One person said that her semi-senile father had mailed more than $45,000 in response to a solicitation.

"For me," he says, "it just seemed logical to turn the table on these people."

PUTTING SPAMMERS ON THE RECEIVING END

Most people have a tough time remembering when they were last in the market for penis-enhancement pills. Yet countless offers for the pills show up in our e-mail boxes virtually every day.

Francis Uy grew tired of these offers and the spammers who made a business out of sending them.

So in 2002, after doing a little digging to find the home address and phone number of a known spammer, Uy posted the information on his own antispam Web site. Within days, the spammer was bombarded with junk mail and unwanted calls. "Spammers make things miserable for the rest of us," says Uy, who is thirty-six and works in the Internet technology department at Johns Hopkins University in Baltimore. "In terms of used bandwidth and storage space, spam puts the cost on recipients rather than on the spammer."

It didn't take long before the spammer came calling and he demanded that Uy remove his personal information from the Web site. "I said absolutely not," Uy recalls.

Instead, Uy posted a note about the call from the spammer on an antispam newsgroup, which caused the spammer to get hit with a new wave of unwanted mail and calls.

"At no point did I explicitly encourage people to

target the spammer," Uy is careful to point out. "That would probably be against the law."

Still, the next time Uy heard from the spammer it was in the form of legal papers notifying him that he was being sued.

Uy's reaction: let the newsgroup know. Once again, he posted a note to his antispammer friends about the lawsuit. In turn, the spammer was hit with yet another round of unsolicited calls and mailings.

When the case finally went to court, the judge ruled in Uy's favor. "He simply said that the information he had posted was public," Uy recounts.

But that was not the end of it because the spammer's luck only got worse. With all the media attention directed at the back-and-forth between Uy and the spammer, AOL took notice and sued the spammer for having used its service for spamming. This case was settled out of court.

"I didn't hear from him for quite a while after that," Uy says. But then one day he got an e-mail from the spammer. "He explained that he was no longer spamming and he asked if I could remove his information from my site," Uy says. "I was happy to accommodate."

MAD LIBS AS REVENGE TOOL

As a kid, Mark Frauenfelder loved to play Mad Libs. As an adult, he turned the game into an unusually effective weapon for getting back at spammers.

It all started after Frauenfelder received a piece of spam selling water filters. The e-mail said: "Do you drink bottled water? Are you looking for a discount? How about 4 cents a gallon? With our high quality water-filtration systems, you can bottle your own!! E-mail your name, address, phone# & e-mail address to The Water Lady—TheWaterLady@——.com."

As a joke, Frauenfelder decided to copy the text of the e-mail into his word processing program and using the "search and replace" function, he substituted every mention of the word "water" with the word "urine."

E-mailing the spammer back, Frauenfelder included his altered text and asked indignantly what the meaning of it was. He said that he was offended by the content and demanded that she explain why she was disseminating such material.

Within hours, she e-mailed back with a confused apology, and she explained that her original e-mail had been altered.

Pleased with the results of his prank, Frauenfelder forwarded his correspondence to several of his friends.

Before long, the text of his mutated e-mail ended up on several sex fetish Web sites.

"I realized I had come across something with real potential," says the forty-four-year-old magazine editor from Los Angeles. He began replying to virtually every spam he received that included an e-mail address.

"More often than not, they responded and were pretty confused and apologetic," he says. "They also seemed serious about trying to figure out who was sabotaging their advertisements."

The spammers soon caught on. Few include their e-mail addresses in what they send out. But Frauenfelder has persisted. He explains that he now resorts to other ways to find the spammers' e-mail addresses, such as looking up their domain name and using free online databanks to find their contact information. As a last resort, he has even looked up the spammers' mailing addresses and has mailed handwritten letters inquiring about the odd e-mail he says he has received from them.

"It's rare that you get the chance to turn this around on them like this," he says.

THE BEAUTY OF WRONG TURNS ON
THE INFORMATION SUPERHIGHWAY

Things move fast on the information superhighway. But it all comes to a screeching halt when you run into a 404.

"Page Not Found (HTTP 404)" is what is displayed when Internet users take a wrong turn or they arrive at a page that is no longer there. These dead pages signal all that is fleeting about the Web: here today, your favorite watering hole could just as soon disappear tomorrow. And what will be left in its stead provides neither sympathy nor a road map for finding your desired location.

"For many people these are disorienting and confusing places," says Jenni Ripley, a thirty-year-old Web developer from Minneapolis. "They are mistakes, not desired destinations."

For Ripley, her first encounter with a 404 was a bittersweet experience.

As a novice Web developer, she had grown dependent on a specific Web page that included a range of useful, though obscure, codes that she needed for a certain type of programming. Then suddenly one day, she tried to visit the page, but it was gone.

"It was jarring to see it missing," she said.

But rather than the typically sparse 404 message,

the dead page offered an interesting alternative. It was a haiku that read:

I ate your web page.
Forgive me, it was juicy
And tart on my tongue.

Though disappointed by the loss of her favorite resource, Ripley was nonetheless tickled. "It struck me as a really interesting idea," she says. "Why not plant something different at this dead end where there is usually only frustration?"

So she wrote an ode to these lonely nooks, elaborating her newfound opinion of 404s as being woefully underappreciated locations. She posted the essay on her personal Web site. Suddenly, a flood of e-mails started arriving. "Many people agreed that 404s can be more than just the result of wrong turns," Ripley says.

To back up this view, many people sent links to dead pages featuring something more than the standard script. Some offered jokes and sarcastic letters to the inadvertent visitor. Others contained video games and odd questionnaires. Many contained photography and poetry.

"To me it was the perfect transformation," says Ripley, who has collected the material at a Web site she created called the 404 Research Lab. "Yes, there's still frustration in these places, but now there's something more as well."

THE INVISIBLE HAND

Maybe it's the sense of panic and frustration that precedes most of the calls. But for whatever reason, when people dial tech support for help they often turn into complete monsters.

Jason Andreas remembers one of his most trying callers.

"The caller said, 'Oh, you're Scottish. Well, that explains a lot since you haven't a clue about what you're doing,'" recounts Andreas, who has worked at a tech-support call center for more than five years. "And this was the same guy who had been transferred to me because he refused to get phone help from 'those dirty Indians.'"

Andreas says that he is always polite to these callers. He avoids jargon at all costs, he adds, because there is no reason to confuse people more.

"I make a point of treating the pushy ones gently," he says, "even when they don't deserve it."

Still, everyone has a breaking point. When callers cross that line, Andreas writes down their user name. And every couple of weeks or so he scrambles their passwords.

The especially egregious callers get additional punishment. "We try to design it specifically for that person," he says.

So the man who kept saying racist things about Muslims found himself signed up to the e-mailing list of Radio Ramadan, a popular Muslim radio show in Scotland. The screaming caller who indicated in the course of one of his rants that he had conservative politics was mysteriously subscribed every week to a new liberal e-mail group.

"The best thing about the tactics," Andreas says, "is that we can check on their effect." He explains that all the help-line technicians at his company can check on people's accounts and read the notes that have been posted about their calls for help.

"A couple days after the scramble, I would check up on my list," he says. "I'd see something like: 'The customer called and was extremely frustrated that for the fourth time in two weeks he had been locked out of his account.' "

WHEN COMMON SENSE STOPS AT THE WRIST

Last week she forwarded the e-mail about flesh-eating bacteria that comes on bananas shipped from Costa Rica. "If you have eaten a banana in the last 2-3 days and come down with a fever followed by a skin infection, seek medical attention!!!" it said.

This week, she forwarded a plea from a seven-year-old dying of lung cancer. It explained that for each person who signs the list, a large foundation would donate seven cents to the little girl's treatment. "The doctors say I will die soon if this isn't fixed, and my family can't pay the bills," the plea said.

We all have at least one person, if not more, in our life who deserves to have her e-mail-forwarding privileges revoked. Usually, these are otherwise intelligent people whose common sense somehow seems to stop at their wrist. Without the slightest bit of discernment, they click to forward us this year's "Top Ten Blond Jokes" or the most recent hackneyed reflection about stopping to smell the roses.

Jeff Zickgraff knows about five of these people, and one week they all seemed to join forces. "I received the same chain e-mail from each of them," he says. "I couldn't believe that so many people were passing along something so stupid."

The e-mail originated from Microsoft and said that the company was testing a new e-mail tracking system. "For each person you send this e-mail to you will be given $5," it promised. "Please forward this on to as many people as possible so that both you and I can take part." Of course, Microsoft was performing no such test and the letter is a hoax that has been around for years. But Zickgraff's friends weren't taking any chances, so they diligently forwarded it along.

Zickgraff, on the other hand, wasn't buying it. "People figure, I'd better be safe and send this along," he says. "But they should probably stop and think about whether it is a hoax and whether they should be helping to promote it." With a few clicks, Zickgraff, who works for a small software start-up company in Indianapolis, found a Web site that verified his suspicions about the supposed Microsoft giveaway.

So he decided to teach his gullible friends a lesson.

Lifting insignias from Microsoft's Web site, he designed company stationery and checks for several hundred dollars. Then he mailed them to everyone who had forwarded him the e-mail.

"You are receiving the enclosed check because you have forwarded one of the selected messages to your friends and family," the letter said. "Again, thank you for your participation in our ongoing research. Please tell your friends and family members that you have been rewarded and that indeed, it does pay to forward our e-mails on to new recipients."

Some of Zickgraff's friends said that they planned to deposit the check. Others just took it around the office bragging to everyone who had been skeptical, he recalls.

"I designed it pretty well but I was surprised that they fell for it," Zickgraff says. "Then again, these are the same people who fell for the original e-mail."

After several delicious days basking in his friends' foolishness, Zickgraff finally fessed up. He directed one friend's attention to the fine print on the back of the check. It said, "Please endorse only in your dreams."

Ross Patty never received the Microsoft chain letter or one of Zickgraff's checks. But he did receive plenty of other chain letters, and often they were the threatening and superstitious kind.

"The world is a nasty enough place already not to need some e-mail coming your way saying that you will be plagued by decades of bad luck if you don't forward it along," says Patty, who is thirty years old and works in tech support at Colorado State University in Fort Collins. "Aside from being bullying, the letters are also so idiotic in what they cite will happen to people who do not forward them."

So Patty decided to write a chain letter of his own, spoofing the genre.

After stating that the letter would have no effect on the recipient's destiny whatsoever, Patty, in keeping with the genre, then walked the reader through a detailed proof of his point.

"For example, Linda Mathews of Birmingham, Alabama, did not receive this letter, and her life continued from that moment totally unaffected," the letter reassured. "On the other hand, Christopher Hill of Detroit, Michigan, did receive this letter. He did not send it on, and received a raise, which had nothing to do with this letter." And on the examples went, with a final line reading, "Now the letter has come to you, and you have the opportunity to pass it on, if you so desire, though you have no real reason to send it to six other people."

Patty says that he has kept the letter on his computer; whenever a friend e-mails him a chain letter, he sends it as a reply.

The irony of it all, he says, is that word got around and several of his friends have asked him for copies so they can begin forwarding it to people. "I'm just waiting for my grandparents or someone else that didn't get it from me to forward it my way," he says. "That's when I know that I've created a monster."

THE LEGAL IMPLICATIONS OF JUST SAYING "HI"

As an increasingly common fixture of modern communication, the e-mail disclaimer has added a litigiousness to even the simplest correspondence. It is not unusual that a one-word e-mail will come with 700 additional words of legalese at the bottom, explaining the confidentiality of the missive and threatening action for any devious uses of it.

In 2001 the trend of e-mail disclaimers had become such a problem that a British technology Web site, The Register, conducted a competition to find the longest disclaimer. The winner was a Swiss investment bank, whose e-mail system automatically added a staggering 1,081-word disclaimer to all e-mails sent from company computers.

"From what we've seen so far, these don't stand up in court," says Jeffrey Goldberg, a network programmer for Cranfield University in England, who runs a Web site dedicated to the topic of e-mail disclaimers. "There is this odd faith that people put in these disclaimers."

Aside from being on shaky legal ground, the disclaimers are often inherently contradictory. Goldberg cited several disclaimers that he had been e-mailed, which stressed the confidentiality of a particular e-mail while also warning that if the e-mail recipient received the e-mail erroneously, he should not open or copy it.

"Of course, the only way you could have read the disclaimer is by opening the e-mail in the first place," Goldberg pointed out.

John S. Allen grew fed up with the disclaimers after someone on a public Listserv kept posting messages from a work e-mail account. The messages always came with elaborate language at the bottom stating that the material in the e-mail was for private consumption only and would result in legal penalties if showed to anyone else.

"Yet here he was posting messages from this e-mail on the public listserve, probably not realizing that the disclaimer was there," says Allen, a fifty-nine-year-old writer based in Waltham, Massachusetts. "I found it more absurd than annoying."

So Allen wrote a disclaimer of his own. It read:

The information contained in this e-mail is being sent out to a list with a hundred or more subscribers. It is archived in two different locations where anyone can read it. Nonetheless, somehow my e-mail software always posts this warning that it may be confidential and is intended solely for the use of the named addressee—and that access, copying or re-use of the e-mail or any information contained therein by any other person is not authorized. Yeah, right, and a restraining order also had been issued against dande-

lion seeds' blowing in the wind. (Just thought I'd remind you all that warmer weather *will* arrive one day fairly soon.)

If you are not the intended recipient, and actually can take any of this seriously, please notify us immediately by returning the e-mail to the originator. That we have not been receiving any such messages indicates the need for an effective, automated monitoring, reporting and penal system to quell such abuse, or preferably, for a good laugh and reconfiguration of the software to eliminate this silly disclaimer.

Since few people ever read the fine print in e-mails, the spoof was missed by most people on the Listserv, Allen says. "But those who noticed certainly got the point," he adds.

RETURN TO SENDER

One of the luxuries of e-mailing is that it allows the recipient to decide when and whether to read certain messages. But if the sender of an e-mail activates the "read receipt" function, an automatic note goes back to the sender right after an e-mail has been read. Dave Mansfield considers this an imposition.

"I don't see why a person has to overstep the line that is built into the way that e-mail is supposed to work," says the twenty-four-year-old data officer for a housing association in London. "This is a complete invasion of my privacy."

Most e-mail systems have a pop-up window that offers the recipient a chance to block the receipt function before the receipt is sent. But Mansfield says that this is little consolation since it's the principle of the matter at stake. "They shouldn't be trying to intrude in the first place," he says.

After a close friend made a habit of using the "read receipt" on all of her outgoing e-mails, Mansfield decided to teach her a lesson. Since he backs up all of his correspondence by having his e-mail sent in duplicate to a second e-mail account, Mansfield waited until the end of each month. He would then go into his back-up account and reopen all of the woman's e-mails. "It would flood her inbox with a month's worth of her receipts," he says.

"I know the tactic got to her," he adds, "because this woman is now my girlfriend and I heard her reasoning in eventually deciding to turn the function off."

8

❦

BILLS, BANKS, AND BILE

No one likes handing over their own hard-earned money, especially when it goes to an institution that already has millions. If you could even read the bill and understand how they came up with some of the charges, it might not be so bad. The most galling part, however, is the hypocrisy. The company takes an eternity to fix your problem. But if you dawdle even slightly with your pay-ment, the threatening letters and fines arrive with lightning speed.

And yet no one wants his electricity or phone service turned off. So while you might grumble a bit, you pay what they tell you to pay, when they tell you to pay it, and how they tell you to pay it.

Then there are those other people. They pay—but they throw in a little something extra, just for good measure. Sometimes it gums up the works. Other times it's just a way to get their opinion across.

Whether they hit their targets or not, these people take what the companies refuse to give: a tiny and satisfying dose of relief.

UNBALANCING THE BOOKS

Nothing in life is free—least of all revenge. But for some, the cost makes no sense, except when you consider the catharsis.

Tom Rentschler has a love for round numbers and a hatred of his phone company. One day he decided to combine the two.

Rentschler says that as a child he was never very good in math class. When it came time to open a checking account, he occasionally rounded numbers up to the nearest dollar to make it easier on himself when balancing his checkbook.

"I just hated doing the counting on small change," says the twenty-nine-year-old high school multimedia teacher from Columbia City, Indiana. But he never imagined that his arithmetic inadequacies would actually work as a weapon.

Then one day he found himself in an argument with his cell phone company about fees and payments due. In the end, Rentschler acquiesced to the charges and asked the phone company to put the charges on his credit card.

"For the sake of clarity I asked the operator to charge $50 rather than the $49.32 that was actually owed on the bill," he says. The operator paused and responded, "Sir, could you please pay the exact amount owed rather than more than that amount?" She explained that otherwise it would add an unnecessary step to the process as the billing department would have to add a credit to his account.

"Is that right? More work for your billing department?" Rentschler remembers thinking before insisting that the operator put a rounded charge for $50 on his credit card. From that moment forward, Rentschler began writing all his bills to the phone company rounded up to the nearest dollar. "I figured: why should I do the math and pass up the chance to stick it to this company," he says. "Let them work it out. It's the least they can do for all the mystery fees they charge."

Chris Buck takes a similar approach, but his enemies are the big oil companies. They frustrate him because they are making millions of dollars in profits while also constantly raising prices at the pumps.

So Buck tries to stay one step ahead of them. When he prepays at gas stations, he leaves a few cents credit.

"Who knows, but I'm pretty sure that the books don't jibe at the end of the day," says Buck, a thirty-eight-year-old communications technician from Washington, D.C.

Irrational? Probably. But he says it still makes him feel better. "I figure that if the gas station attendant spends more than ten seconds figuring out my transaction," he says, "then that may add up to twelve minutes per year."

A few cents is worth it, he adds, if it helps unbalance the books.

LIKE KRYPTONITE FOR BANK CHECKS

First the bank increased his checking fees and added new ones that made no sense. Then it changed its policy so that customers could no longer "float" checks. That meant they could no longer write a check with a future date on it so that the bank would have to wait a while before depositing it. But the last straw for Chris Anders was when the bank automated its check processing so that checks began clearing within hours rather than days.

"They leave us no wiggle room when finances are tight," says Anders, a thirty-seven-year-old manager at an Internet technology firm in Atlanta. "All they are interested in is efficiency and getting their hands on our money so that they can start earning their interest on it."

So Anders devised a way to slow their process down.

At the bottom of every check is a string of numbers. Printed in magnetic ink, these numbers allow check-scanning machines to read the check instantly and digitally move the money from one checking account to another, he says. But if the magnetism of the ink does not work, the machines have difficulty running the checks and they have to be handled manually.

Anders loves when that happens.

"The magnet I use takes two hands to pull it off the

refrigerator," he says. He keeps it on the corner of his desk and every time he writes a check, he drags the magnet across the bottom of it. "I have no way of knowing how well it works, if at all," he says. "But it's still worth doing."

MAKING THE LATE-PAYMENT NOTICE
WORK FOR YOU

It is only a couple days past the bill's due date and already the phone company has sent a stern notice.

"It's ridiculous," says Suzy Green. "You have to be patient with them when service is down but they start making threats within no time."

Green said she used to get nervous about these letters. Now she embraces them. Realizing that most companies rarely take action before issuing several warnings, she waits for at least one of these notices to arrive before she makes her payment.

"The key is to find the balance," says Green, a thirty-eight-year-old Web developer from Alameda, California. "You have to figure out how many days late is not so late that they shut off the service but is still late enough that they have to send a second notice."

Green says that she does not deal with all her bills this way, just the ones that go to companies that are rigid with payment deadlines.

"They make it part of their system to bother you to get you to cooperate," she said. "So I make it part of my system to bother them back."

GIVING HIS TWO CENTS
AND GETTING SOMETHING BACK

When Brian Decker decided to take a swipe at his city's parking authority, he discovered that sometimes these faceless adversaries swipe back.

After parking his car in a garage in Palo Alto, California, one afternoon, Decker returned to find that he had received a ticket for $20. Apparently, he had parked in a garage that was for "authorized vehicles only." So Decker sent a letter to the parking authority contesting the ticket, arguing that there were no clear signs indicating that the garage was restricted. But a representative from the authority replied that it was too late to contest the citation, and he informed Decker that he now also owed a late fee for an additional $20.

Fuming, Decker wrote back. "Past the date to contest a citation? Past the date to enact justice?" he asked. "Here is your dirty money." He included a check for $40.02, figuring that by overpaying by two cents he would force the authority to spend an extra thirty-four cents (which was the postal rate at the time) for the stamp required to mail him back his refund.

"I had heard this urban legend that if you slightly overpay tickets, it prevents them from closing the account until they've issued a refund, which gums up the system," says Decker, who is now a law student at the University of Pennsylvania. "I thought I'd test it out."

A month later his refund arrived: two pennies taped to a receipt. Decker was ecstatic, and he figured that was the end of it. Proud of his victory, he showed the refund letter to all his friends.

But then came another letter. This one was from a collections agency.

It stated that Decker still owed the city money. After calling the collections agency to explain that he had already paid the city for the ticket and late fees, Decker was told that an official from the city would have to contact the collections agency to verify his payment.

Yet again, Decker wrote to the parking authority. Not only did he implore them to verify with the collections agency that he had already paid, but he also instructed the city to repay him for the postage and expenses he had incurred in dealing with the collections agency. "The bill for postage on that letter [to the collections agency] comes to a total of $0.34, as does the postage on this letter," he wrote. "In addition, I was charged $0.17 for the two copies I made at Kinko's. The expenses are outlined below: Postage for letter to PRS $0.34, Postage for this letter $0.34, Copies from Kinko's $0.17, Total $0.85."

The city created the problem with the collections

agency, he argued, so the city should pay for dealing with it.

Days and then weeks passed. No response arrived. So Decker did what the city would have done: he sent another letter, upping the ante. "I have neither received a response from you nor the payment ($0.85) due," he wrote. "Please consider this a second notice."

Explaining the fees he had already levied, Decker then increased the total amount due, adding in the cost of the postage and copying expenses for the second letter. "In addition, late charges of $2.15 are now due because no payment was received within thirty days," he wrote.

Decker never received his money. He says that he doubts he ever will. Just in case, however, he says that he is considering taking the matter to the next level.

"I'm thinking that I may need to resort to a collections agency," he says. "But I'm still hoping we can work this out amicably."

WHEN FRUSTRATION
BECOMES A CLASS PROJECT

As a student in business school, Jim McManus figured that he, more than anyone, should be able to understand the fees that appeared on his monthly bank statement.

But he couldn't.

The names of the fees were too nondescript. Who honestly knows what a "user service charge" or a "processing fee" really means?

McManus says that the most perplexing part was the bank's decision to raise the amount of money he needed to have in his account to qualify for free checking. He wrote to the bank's vice president asking for an explanation, but what came back was even more confusing and circuitous.

So he turned to his peers. At the time, he was enrolled in a class where the students were discussing business ethics and regulations. He presented the bank's letter and asked if the ten or so other classmates would write a couple of paragraphs analyzing which fees were legal and which were ethical. He sent the resulting stack of letters back to the bank's vice president with a cover sheet explaining that his group was reviewing the matter.

"I got a call back within days," says McManus,

who is now forty-five years old and works as a software researcher at a university in Virginia. The bank's lawyer began asking in what direction McManus planned on taking his project and why he had gotten others involved. "In the end, none of the fees were ever lifted and I only got a partial explanation of them," he says. "But the nervousness in the lawyer's voice was worth every cent."

NO COMMENT

The bills are high and rising, but there is often no alternative provider to your local utility company. So Scott Randall's strategy is to try to kill 'em with kindness.

When Randall gets his gas bill from the Sacramento Municipal Utilities District, he marvels that the prices keep rising. It is often only a couple cents but it adds up over time. Since the utility holds a virtual monopoly in his area, he says his options are limited.

But rather than just stewing about it, Randall, who is an air pollution specialist for the Environmental Protection Agency, writes a small note just above the portion of the bill that says, "Please do not write comments on this bill."

He started doing this several years ago after a friend who worked for the utility company told him that the computers that process the bills get tripped up every time they come across unrecognizable text.

"Your energy tastes the best!" he writes, or "You Rock!" Just like the slow creep of the price increases, he says that he believes over time his tactics will gradually add up in costs for the utility company.

"You get back at them in the ways you can," he says.

THE LITTLE JAB THAT WOKE UP A GOLIATH

They usually come packaged in lofty promises. "Try our business model and this money is as good as yours!" or "We will save you so much money that we might as well just give it to you now." Sending fake checks is a standard marketing ploy. The checks are made to look real to grab our attention, at least until we recognize the scheme and move on.

But Patrick Combs did not move on. He took his ersatz check to the bank and days later the check cleared, all $95,093.35 of it.

"I've always hated these checks," says Combs, who is thirty-eight and lives in San Diego. "They're total come-ons and they're designed to mislead us."

Though it began as a joke, Combs's saga quickly turned into an epic struggle against his bank as he tried to make a larger point about the way businesses treat people.

The fake check, from a get-rich-quick scheme, looked entirely real except for the words "Non-Negotiable For Cash" typed on the top right-hand corner. "It's obvious to you or me," says Combs. "But elderly people and non-native speakers of English fall for these things all the time."

So he drew a smiley face on the back as his endorsement signature and deposited it through his ATM. "It was a tiny way to poke fun," he says.

Several days later, when he saw that his account had jumped from four to six figures, he called a banker friend for his opinion of the situation. The friend explained that the numbers were only a credit until the check cleared.

"Don't get excited," the friend said. "The numbers will disappear in a day or so."

But they didn't. Days and then weeks went by and the six figures remained.

So Combs started investigating. He called a bank representative and asked how long it takes after a check is deposited before the money becomes officially and irreversibly his own.

"Legally, it's ten days," the representative said. Three weeks had already passed.

Next, Combs asked a person at another department of the bank.

"Actually, it is only twenty-four hours," this person told him. "That's the law," he said.

After that, Combs headed to his local law library to research the issue himself. The law book he found said twenty-four hours. The words "non-negotiable," the law book also said, are not sufficient to invalidate a check.

"Still, I felt like the rug would be pulled from under me at any moment," Combs recalls. As an added precaution, he withdrew the money as a money order and placed it in a safety deposit box at his bank.

Then came the call he had been expecting for weeks. In a stern and raspy voice, the director of bank security told Combs that he needed to return the money immediately. "If you don't," the man said, "I'll be visiting you in jail."

But Combs had done his homework, so he was not easily intimidated. He said that he had broken no law. And, he argued, it was the bank that had erred in clearing the check rather than bouncing it within twenty-four hours, as was its responsibility. A debate ensued which dragged on for weeks. "He kept telling me to hand over the check," Combs says. "I kept telling him no."

In the meantime, Combs kept researching the law and grew increasingly confident about his position. But the more he thought about keeping the money, the less comfortable he was with the idea. "I realized that if I kept it, I would become exactly what I hated most about banks in general," he says. "They set up a system in which they never cut you a break and they never give leniency for small mistakes, and here I would be doing the same thing."

Finally, Combs decided what to do: he told the bank that if it admitted its mistake, and it did so in writing, he would return all of the money.

"It wasn't much to ask for," he says.

For the bank, Combs's ultimatum represented the ultimate game of chance. If the bank agreed to write the letter, it would create a document that could easily be used against it. But if the bank didn't acquiesce, the matter would likely go to court, where Combs felt he already had the upper hand.

Four months passed while the bank vacillated over what to do. Finally, Combs got his letter. And the bank got its money back.

"To me it was a victory worth a lot more than $95,000," he says. "Who ever actually gets a bank to admit they're wrong?"

Several weeks after receiving his letter from the bank, Combs was asked to close his account. "I thought it was really a slap in the face," he says. Several weeks after that, the bank closed permanently.

Combs now works as a consultant to banks and other large businesses, advising them about customer service concerns. He has also turned his story into a one-man stage routine called "Man 1, Bank 0." His routine is playing off-Broadway this year.

9

TURNABOUT IS FAIR PLAY

It's a simple and age-old concept: an eye for an eye and a tooth for a tooth.

But aside from leaving us all blind and tooth-less, this form of justice becomes truly ridiculous when applied to the most mundane grievances. Still, the payoff is sometimes too tempting to pass up.

And why should we?

Who said it's not fair to offer something back to the Jehovah's Witness who keeps showing up at our door? Why not regift the regifter or get uppity about English pronunciation when dealing with the French?

Karma hardly seems worth it, if we have to wait for the next life to reap its rewards. The prudent people are those who even the score now.

REGIFTING AS TACTIC AND ANNOYANCE

A book about gardening, and you live in an apartment. A New Age compilation, but you prefer classic rock. A loaf of fruit bread.

Unwanted gifts are tedious not just because of the feigned delight required in receiving them, but also because they present a difficult question: What do you do with gifts you don't want? Having them further clutter up your space is not a great option, but can you really bear to throw away something that is brand new?

These items are even worse when they come with that certain stale whiff of having been regifted. And when this happens, the natural instinct is to try to pass it off onto someone else.

That's when it starts getting ugly.

Martin Wade knows this predicament all too well. After a close friend had been talking for a while about taking up bowling as a hobby, Wade gave him a high-quality bowling ball for his birthday. Several years later, the friend gave him the same ball back as a Christmas present.

"He had completely forgotten that I gave it to him," says Wade, who is fifty-seven years old and owns a carpet-cleaning business in Jackson, Mississippi.

Not to be outdone, Wade took the ball to a local bowling alley, where he had a single large hole drilled in the center. Taking the ball home, he then used his power sander to flatten its bottom. When the friend's wife had her next birthday, Wade filled the hole with a bouquet of flowers and presented it to her as a vase.

"Not only did I never get the ball back again," Wade says with a boyish chuckle. "But it gave me the opportunity to give them a matching, perfectly hideous lamp made from a bowling pin on my friend's next birthday."

FORGETTING TO TURN OFF
THE ALARM CLOCK

Few college students like to be woken up at 7 a.m. on a Saturday. For Erik Costlow it was a weekly ritual.

Costlow's college roommate used to go home on the weekends to visit his girlfriend, but he had a habit of forgetting to turn off his alarm clock.

"It yanked me from a dead sleep," says Costlow, who attended Illinois State University and now works as a computer programmer. "It was a pretty loud beeping that you couldn't possibly sleep through." He asked the roommate to write a note reminding himself to turn off the clock before leaving for the weekend. That didn't work.

So Mr. Costlow and his friends decided to give the roommate a taste of his own medicine. Removing the faceplate of the clock, Costlow, who had taken courses in high school on electrical engineering, found a wire that could be reconnected to make the clock function on the level of electrical current that is often found in European electrical outlets. Connecting the wire but continuing to run the clock on an American electrical outlet meant that it would run much faster.

"It functioned as though there were only fifty seconds in a minute," Costlow explains.

After returning to school one Sunday night, the

roommate checked the alarm to make sure it was set to wake him up on time the next day. Everything looked to be in working order. But when the alarm went off several hours early the next day, the roommate found himself seated in biology class at 7 a.m. when the class wasn't until 9 o'clock.

"He kept trying to reset the clock each night thinking he had made some mistake and he kept getting burnt," says Costlow. "It was the only time that waking up early was actually something I looked forward to."

THE REMINDER CALL

Perhaps it's well intentioned, but some people still find it condescending.

Doctors hate getting stood up, and rescheduling can often be difficult. As a result, many doctors have their receptionist make a friendly reminder call to patients the day before an appointment.

"What am I, a ten-year-old?" asks Christine Mira, a Vancouver-based Web developer. "I have a calendar and I've never missed an appointment, so stop wasting my time."

The reminders take two forms. One is for an upcoming appointment. The other is when a patient hasn't visited in a while. Dentists tend to send reminder postcards. Physicians seem to prefer phone calls.

Mira says that her chiropractor was especially bad about telling her when she hadn't been in recently enough. "Eventually I got my message through to them that the calls weren't needed," she says.

But it took some effort.

First, Mira politely told the receptionist that she did not need the reminder calls. If there is a lapse in my regular visits, she explained, please just assume it's intentional.

They didn't listen and the calls kept coming.

Then Mira began giving receptionists a cell phone number that she rarely answers. But they kept leaving messages, and clearing the recordings was getting tedious. "I don't quite understand why these offices don't ask you when you first join whether you want reminder calls or not," she says.

Finally, Mira decided that she would beat them at their own game. She would preemptively call the office before her appointment. "Hi, it's Christine," she would say. "I'm just calling to remind you that I will be in to see you tomorrow at 2 p.m. Is that still a good time for you? You'll be there then? Wonderful!"

Eventually, the receptionist got annoyed enough to ask her gently to stop. Mira asked for the same in return, and the two sides declared a truce.

REVERSING THE LANGUAGE SNOBBERY

Having been a French major in college, Robert Koslow prides himself on his ability with the language. So it especially irks him when he visits Paris and the locals force him to speak English. "There is a famous snobbery there about how you speak French," says the fifty-one-year-old real estate consultant. "It has to be perfect or else."

One afternoon while walking in Manhattan, where he lives, Koslow found his chance for payback. A group of French tourists stopped to ask him for directions.

"Where is Fifth Avenue?" one of the tourists asked in accented but perfectly understandable English.

"Excuse me?" Koslow replied.

The tourist repeated his question.

With a blank stare, Koslow switched to French. "Could you say it in French for me, I don't understand," he said.

Puzzled, the tourist asked his question in French.

"Oh, you mean 'Where is Fifth Avenue?' " Koslow said in English with an exasperated laugh. He then pointed the group in the right direction.

Heading on their way, the tourists seemed baffled. "They didn't get it," Koslow said. "Still, it felt good to me."

LOVE THY NEIGHBOR, WHEN HE IS QUIET

Like many big cities, Paris is crowded and noisy. Inconsiderate neighbors are a fact of life. Confronting them about their loud stereo or barking dog can be an intimidating prospect. That's why Ivan Duval's art project is so useful.

"My friends and I are creative people," says the thirty-eight-year-old artist, who lives there. "We figured that it might be artistically and conceptually interesting to create a CD that no one wanted to hear." He called it the Revenge CD, and it features tracks with the sound of a drill, a party of more than two hundred people, walking in high heels, and spring cleaning. Duval has sold more than ten thousand copies—complete with earplugs—since he created it in 2003.

For the more timid types who want to frustrate their neighbor but only gently, the tracks with cooing pigeons and the newborn baby are best, Duval said. "While those sounds can really annoy a neighbor," he says, "they also are sounds that usually don't cause them to come knocking because they figure you cannot do anything about them."

Almost all of the tracks feature recordings that are no longer than two minutes, but most stereos have a repeat function that allows for continual play. "There are people who hate their neighbor so much that they leave their apartment for the weekend and leave a sound playing the whole time," Duval says.

The Revenge CD would have come in handy for Steven Haas.

When an upstairs neighbor began making a habit of blaring his favorite seventies rock station in the evening as Haas was trying to unwind after work, he did not know what to do. He first tried to talk to the neighbor about the matter. This worked for a while. But soon enough, the noise was back. Next, he turned to the landlord, but he was unwilling to intervene. So eventually, Haas decided to put to use some of the electrical engineering skills he had picked up back in college.

He ordered a small wireless FM transmitter starter kit from an electronics hobbyist catalogue. The device, which cost less than $20, enabled a person to tune to a certain frequency and broadcast over the radio. Though the transmitter was a low-powered device and could not broadcast very far, it had the effect of jamming the radio belonging to Haas's neighbor.

Whenever the neighbor played his radio too loud, Haas flipped on his transmitter and, poof, no more noise. When the music cut off, Haas could hear his neighbor swearing in frustration as he got up and stomped across his living room to fidget with the machine.

Invariably, the neighbor would try to raise the volume. So Haas would wait for half a minute and then flip his transmitter back off.

"I could literally hear the guy leap when his radio suddenly came on full blast," says Haas, a fifty-year-old freelance publicist from New York. "I think it was especially enjoyable because the neighbor was an electrical engineer, but he never figured out what was going on, which made it all the more annoying for him."

PAY NOW OR PAY LATER

Rude people are bad. Stingy ones are worse. And at the very bottom are crummy tippers.

Anyone who has worked as a waiter knows the sort of creeps that walk among us and the extent of short-changing that occurs even when service is above par.

"Even if the waiter is a disaster, it makes no sense to shaft on the tip," says Chris Fehlinger, who is thirty-six years old and has worked as a waiter in New York City for more than twelve years. "Since most places pool tips, you end up penalizing the busboys, the bartender, and the other waiters, all of whom are probably hustling."

The smarter and more pinpointed thing to do, Fehlinger explains, is to make a comment to management, which is far more likely to get results, and it will do so without hurting anyone else in the process.

The tougher question, however, is what a waiter can do about skimpy tippers. The problem with trying to achieve revenge in these cases is that by the time the waiter discovers the crime, the culprit is long gone.

This is why Fehlinger came up with the Shitty Tipper Database.

"I've seen a fair share of stingy and obnoxious people," he says. "The database just struck me as something hilarious to do about it."

Featuring the full name of the tightwad, the location of the inadequate tipping, and the exact amount of the tip, and bill (with a percentage calculated so that the reader understands clearly how bad the tip was), the Shitty Tipper Database has more than two thousand listings. "The beauty of it is that lots of people go on Google and do a vanity search to see where their name pops up," says Fehlinger. "And suddenly they see they're in there."

Since creating the Web site in the spring of 1999, Fehlinger has received on average several e-mails and letters per week from people demanding that their name be removed from the list. Few deny the amount of money they left, he said, and most offer some explanation about bad service.

"If they threaten to sue for not removing their name, I usually explain to them that they will have to get a cease-and-desist order first before they can sue and that this piece of paper costs about $300 in legal fees," says Fehlinger, adding that he has yet to be bullied into taking a name off the list. "Then I usually point out that that's about a hundred times the three measly dollars they should have left on the table."

CAR HORNS THAT DOUBLE AS DOORBELLS

To be woken up every morning by the sound of a car horn is bad enough. But when the person honking is doing so as part of their daily carpooling ritual, it can really boil the blood.

"These people are so inconsiderate and lazy that they were unwilling to get out and knock on the front door," says Bart Everson, a thirty-eight-year-old multimedia artist who works at the University of Louisiana in New Orleans. "I had to figure out some way to get back at them."

So whenever an inconsiderate driver pulled up in front of his neighbor's house and honked his horn, Everson used his own car to talk back. "It was just the right level of response for the situation," he says.

Everson drives a 1995 Saturn sedan that comes with a key clicker with two buttons on it. One button opens the doors of the car. The other is for emergencies and triggers a distress alarm by honking the horn repeatedly every several seconds like a car alarm. Whenever the annoying horn honker pulled up, Everson waited for the toot and then he honked back using his remote clicker.

"If you worked it right you could make it honk once, twice, or non-stop," he says. "It was perfect for annoying the guy or just drowning him out."

JEHOVAH'S WITNESS, MEET HARI KRISHNA

Richard Gibbons is too nice to be rude to the people who kept pushing their religion on him, so he began offering a trade instead.

Every two weeks or so, Gibbons gets a knock at his front door from the Jehovah's Witnesses. Gibbons, forty-one, from Nottingham, England, says that he has told them that he is not interested. "But incredibly enough, they keep coming," he says.

Unlike most people, Gibbons thinks it is rude to pretend that he is not at home. When solicitors come knocking, he always opens the door, politely listens to their pitch, and occasionally engages the people in a friendly debate about religion.

Every so often during his lunch break, Gibbons is confronted by Hari Krishnas who work the corners near the offices of his Internet technology firm. Usually he tries to avoid them by crossing the street. If confronted, however, he grits his teeth while politely listening.

"It was getting pretty tiresome," he says.

But recently, Gibbons has been looking forward to seeing the Hari Krishnas and the Jehovah's Witnesses. He rarely crosses the street preemptively anymore. And he also eagerly accepts the reading material offered by the Hari Krishnas.

Whenever the Jehovahs show up, he offers them Krishna reading and asks for them to promise that they will read his literature in exchange for him reading theirs.

"I tell them that we can both explore the competing visions of ultimate truth that are out there," he says. No one has accepted his offer yet, but he said that the visits from the Jehovah's Witnesses have dropped off considerably.

CRASHING THE PARTY

Telemarketing the telemarketers is a beautiful notion. It's even better if you can do it at 3 a.m.

Tom Mabe did just that.

Mabe is not one to shy from passive-aggressive combat; he is, after all, the stand-up comedian from Louisville, Kentucky, who engaged in psychological warfare against his cell phone company. (See page 100.) After finding out about a telemarketers' conference in Washington, D.C., Mabe booked himself into the hotel where it was being held. Waiting until 3 a.m. on the first night, he began dialing other guests in the hotel, almost all of whom were attending the conference.

"I'm calling to offer you a revolutionary new sleeping pill called Sleepy Sleep Aid," he said to some of the people. "If you had already taken this pill you would be asleep right now."

For others, he told them he wanted to offer them long distance for five cents per minute.

"Some people actually took me seriously," he says. "Most of them asked what time it was and told me I was insane."

EPILOGUE

The annoying part of this book is what it lacks. Has no one devised a clever way to get back at recalcitrant movie talkers and loud gum chewers? Isn't there something we can do to those people who gab at the register while the long line behind them waits or to those banks that charge ridiculously high ATM fees? Surely our frustrations have not outstripped our creativity. Stand up and be counted, clever curmudgeons. The cosmic balance is at stake. Join the ranks at: www.lifeslittleannoyances.com.

A NOTE TO THE READER

While the book chronicles the range and diversity of the ways that people respond to life's little annoyances, it is not an endorsement of any single approach and is certainly not intended to recommend, much less to condone, dangerous or illegal activity.

ACKNOWLEDGMENTS

I am indebted to the many people who were willing to reveal themselves to me in all their creative, petty, and vindictive glory. I would never have found them all were it not for Sahar Habibi's speedy legwork and smart research. Mark Thomas and Gunnar Hellekson were also constant sources of good ideas. I am grateful to Christy Fletcher, my agent, for nimbly getting the project started and to Paul Golob, my editor at Times Books, for forcefully steering it on its way—always with good humor and careful dedication. None of it would have been possible without Alex Ward's careful diplomacy and smart editorial input. The hustle and creativity of the team at Henry Holt and Company was equally invaluable.

Thanks especially to Susan Edgerley and Joe Sexton, my bosses at *The New York Times*, for giving me the time I needed and the support I could never have expected. My gratitude goes to Wendell Jamieson, who worked his standard magic on my prose in the original piece. I also appreciate Kevin Flynn for tireless mentorship and Gerry Mullany for constantly being so flexible.

Most especially, thanks go to Sherry and Amanda for sharing with me a perspective on the world and for picking up so much slack as I try to offer a piece of this perspective to others.

ABOUT THE AUTHOR

IAN URBINA is a reporter for *The New York Times*, based in the paper's Washington bureau. He has degrees in history from Georgetown University and the University of Chicago, and his writings, which range from domestic and foreign policy to commentary on everyday life, have appeared in the *Los Angeles Times*, *The Guardian*, *Harper's Magazine*, and elsewhere. He lives in Washington, D.C., with his wife, son, stepdaughter, and a nuisance of a dog.